As one of th...
a...
Thomas Coo... are the experts in travel.

For more than 135 years our
guidebooks have unlocked the secrets
of destinations around th...
sharing with travellers a w...
experience and a passion fo...

Rely on Thomas Coo...
travelling companion on your...
and benefit from our unique heritage.

Thomas Cook **traveller** guides

ANDALUCÍA
INCLUDING SEVILLE
Thomas Cook Authors &
Nick Inman

Your travelling companion since 1873

Written by Thomas Cook authors and Nick Inman,
updated by Nick Inman and Clara Villanueva
Original photography by Michelle Chaplow

Published by Thomas Cook Publishing
A division of Thomas Cook Tour Operations Limited
Company registration no. 3772199 England
The Thomas Cook Business Park, Unit 9, Coningsby Road,
Peterborough PE3 8SB, United Kingdom
Email: books@thomascook.com, Tel: + 44 (0) 1733 416477
www.thomascookpublishing.com

Produced by Cambridge Publishing Management Limited
Burr Elm Court, Main Street, Caldecote CB23 7NU
www.cambridgepm.co.uk

ISBN: 978-1-84848-338-5

© 2005, 2007, 2009 Thomas Cook Publishing
This fourth edition © 2011
Text © Thomas Cook Publishing
Maps © Thomas Cook Publishing/PCGraphics (UK) Limited

Series Editor: Karen Beaulah
Production/DTP: Steven Collins

Printed and bound in Spain by GraphyCems

Cover photography: © Shaun Egan/Getty Images

Contents

Introduction

Stretching from the shores of the Atlantic to the coast of the Mediterranean, Andalucía is one of Spain's largest regions and, arguably, its most diverse and fascinating. Its landscapes range from 'wild west' desert in the east to temperate rainforests in the west; and its settlements from high-rise holiday resorts on the Costa del Sol to isolated villages in the mountains of the interior. The region's three big cities, Seville (the capital), Córdoba and Granada, are indelibly marked by the civilisation of Muslim Spain.

The sheer extent and amount of Andalucía's history and culture can be overwhelming. Enigmatic dolmens, cave paintings and excavated architectural sites across the region give us a glimpse of the intelligent, creative peoples who were living here up to 25,000 years ago.

Gradually, the natural riches of southern Spain began to attract the attention of the trading nations of the Mediterranean. The Phoenicians are believed to have founded Cádiz, Europe's oldest town, in 1100 BC. From the end of the 3rd century BC Andalucía formed an important part of the Roman Empire, as can be seen particularly at Italica outside Seville, which was founded in 206 BC.

Despite being isolated at the southwesternmost tip of Europe, Andalucía did not escape the Visigoth invasions of the 4th century AD. Converted to Christianity, the northern invaders turned Seville into a centre for learning, trade and culture.

The Visigoths were themselves supplanted in AD 711 by the arrival of the North African Moors, who spread swiftly through the region and left an indelible impression on its cities, landscape and culture. Water technologies introduced by the Moors transformed the near-desert landscape of most of the region, and the new rulers appear to have been comparatively enlightened, allowing both Christians and Jews to practise their trades and religions.

As the Moorish influence fanned out across the Iberian peninsula, stretching beyond what is now Barcelona on the Mediterranean coast and almost as far as the modern Portuguese border on the Atlantic coast, the region's disparate Catholic kingdoms, confined to the north by the Moorish invasion, began to take their lands back. The Reconquest of Spain, launched in the 11th century, pushed the Moors back south, until the last Moorish king, Boabdil, fled Granada in 1492.

With the *Reyes Católicos*, the Catholic kings, in the ascendant, Seville was ideally positioned for the golden age of Spanish expansionism. By the beginning of the 16th century it was the centre of all trade with the new territories in the Americas. As trade with the Americas declined in subsequent centuries, however, and Spain lost her colonies to independence movements, the economy of Andalucía slumped and the region became Spain's poor, long-suffering south. Only in recent decades, with the restitution of democracy and Spain's entry into the EU, has Andalucía become revitalised and determined to make the most of its many and varied attractions for modern tourists.

La Giralda tower in Seville

The region

The provinces of Andalucía – Seville, Huelva, Cádiz, Málaga, Córdoba, Jaén, Granada and Almería – represent almost every type of terrain you might encounter in Spain: from marshland to the highest mountain on mainland Spain; from rolling temperate farmland, sandy orange groves and olive plantations to bleak lunar desert and fantastical dune systems; and from the congested beaches of the Mediterranean to the wild and empty strands of the Atlantic Costa de la Luz.

Andalucía covers 17.3 per cent of the surface area of Spain, making it larger than Ireland, Denmark or Switzerland. With over 8 million inhabitants, it is the most populous Spanish region.

It is separated from the rest of Spain by the formidable mountain chain of the Sierra Morena and runs up to the border with Portugal in the west. It has coasts on both the Atlantic and the Mediterranean. North Africa (Morocco) is just 15km (9 miles) away at its closest point across the Strait of Gibraltar.

The landscape is extraordinarily varied, ranging from the bleak peak of Mulhacén (3,478m/11,471ft), the highest summit in the Iberian peninsula, to the densely built-up resorts of the Costa del Sol. Andalucía's principal river is the Guadalquivir which flows out of the Sierra de Cazorla and through Seville to meet the sea beside Doñana National Park, pride of the region's many nature reserves.

Andalucía missed out on Spain's industrialisation until comparatively recently, and its development was further held back by *latifundismo*, a system of land tenure by which large estates were owned by absentee land-owners and unskilled farm workers were forced to eke out a precarious living as day labourers.

The transition to democracy and Spain's membership of the European Union have brought enormous changes to the region. The most telling sign that Andalucía has caught up with the rest of western Europe is that instead of dispatching its unemployed workforce to distant places to look for work, it has gone full circle and become a magnet for immigration in its own right.

Zahara de los Atunes in Cádiz province

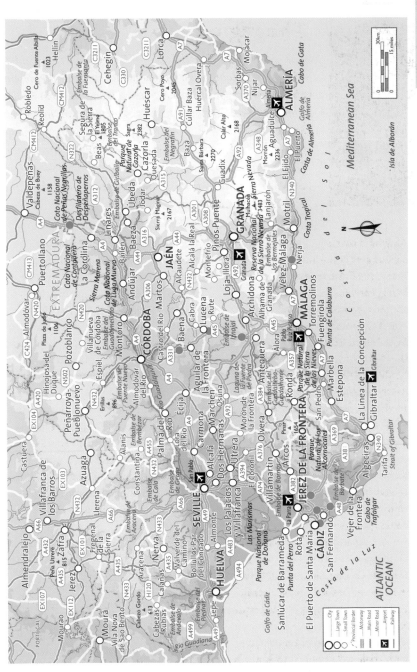

The region

History

30,000 BC Estimated age of Palaeolithic cave drawings found in La Cueva de Pileta, Montejaque, Serranía de Ronda mountains.

15,000–7000 BC Spread of farming and settlements begins to overtake hunter-gatherer cultures, extending from the Fertile Crescent (modern-day Middle East) westwards.

4000 BC Burial mound in Granada province from this date contained clothing, including shoes, religious offerings and other gifts. At roughly the same time, animal husbandry or cattle breeding begins.

2200 BC Bronze Age artefacts from this period found in dolmen burial chambers at Millares, Almería.

1100 BC Founding of Cádiz, said to be Europe's first city, by Phoenician adventurers on lagoon at mouth of Río Guadalete (Guadalete River).

600 BC Greek traders arrive on Mediterranean coast, likely importers of earliest olive trees.

500 BC Carthage colonises southern part of peninsula.

206 BC Romans defeat Carthaginians, begin construction of Italica (5km/3 miles north of modern Seville).

AD 415 Visigoths from northern Europe's modern-day Baltic regions invade Spain.

446 Spain under Visigoth control.

590 First Visigoth conversions to Christianity.

711 Tariq ibn Zayid, governor of Tangier, lands a 10,000-strong Berber army near Tarifa.

756 Independent Moorish emirate declared in Córdoba.

1085 First decisive victory of Catholic Reconquest at Toledo.

1147	Almohads take Seville and regions, begin construction of Torre del Oro and La Giralda tower.
1236	Christians retake Córdoba.
1248	Christians retake Seville.
1469	Marriage of Fernando of Aragon and Isabel of Castilla unites the kingdoms of Castilla and Aragon. Fernando and Isabel pursue the Reconquest with vigour.
1480	Inquisition established in Seville. Among its first victims are homosexuals, Jews and, later, Protestants and Mudéjars (Moors who were 'allowed to stay').
1492	The last Moorish redoubt, Granada, falls to the Christians. Columbus sails for the Americas, funded by the Spanish throne.
1519	Hernán Cortés conquers Peru.
1532	Ferdinand Magellan embarks on the first circumnavigation of the world.
1580	Seville is officially declared the largest city in Spain.
1588	Spanish Armada launches an attack on England but is defeated in the English Channel.
1609	King Felipe III orders expulsion of all Moors from Spain.
1630	Madrid overtakes Seville as the largest city in Spain.
1701–13	War of the Spanish Succession in which the Habsburg kings are supplanted by the Bourbon dynasty through the intervention of France.
1713	Under the Treaty of Utrecht, Britain takes control of Gibraltar.
1717	With the Río Guadalquivir silted and no longer navigable, trade with the Americas moves to Cádiz.
1804–14	Peninsular War (called the War of Independence in Spain) in which British troops under Wellington fight with the Spanish to drive invading French troops out of Spain. At the Battle of Bailen (Jaén) in 1808, Napoleon suffers defeat. Cádiz is besieged by the French but holds out.

1805 Britain defeats the combined fleets of Spain and France at the Battle of Trafalgar off Cape Trafalgar, north of Tarifa.

1811–12 Spanish radicals establish the Cortes, or Spanish Parliament, in Cádiz, under a state of siege. The liberals are defeated by Bourbon king Fernando VII but set a template for a future constitution.

1833 Disputes between conservative Fernando VII and liberal Carlos IV lead to the First Carlist War.

1835 Church property confiscated and sold off.

1846 Second Carlist War.

1872 Third (and final) Carlist War.

1873 Short-lived First Republic established, but founders due to inability to control Spain's regions. Monarchy restored in 1874.

1881 Pablo Picasso born in Málaga.

1882 Worsening conditions for farm workers in western Andalucía, in particular around Seville, lead to increasing unrest.

1895–8 Spain loses Cuba during the US-backed Cuban War.

1910 La Confederación Nacional del Trabajo (National Labour Confederation, or CNT) founded in Seville by embryonic anarchists following Russian theorists such as Mikhail Bakunin.

1917 Start of three years of anarchist uprising across Andalucía.

1923 General Miguel Primo de Rivera stages military coup, winning support with promises to modernise state and economy.

1929 The great Ibero-American Exposition coincides with the Wall Street Crash (30 November).

1930 Effects of the Depression unseat Rivera, who is replaced in 1931 by the Second Republic, riven by factional dispute.

1936 Tensions between the right-wing Falange and the disorganised left-wing

Popular Front break out into open Civil War.

1939	The Civil War ends with defeat for the left. Franco keeps Spain out of World War II, but Spain is boycotted by the UN, forcing the nation, Andalucía particularly, into *los años de hambre* (Years of Hunger), when many starve.
1947	Bullfighter Manolete is killed at Linares.
1969	Gibraltar border closed.
1975	Franco dies. Juan Carlos becomes King Juan Carlos I and reintroduces democracy to Spain.
1982	Spanish Socialist Workers' Party, PSOE, led by Felipe González, is voted into power. Andalucía becomes an autonomous region governed from Seville.
1985	Border with Gibraltar opens.
1986	Spain joins the European Community.
1992	Expo 92 puts Seville and Spain on the world stage.

1994	First high-speed AVE train runs from Madrid to Seville in 2½ hours.
1996	After 14 years of PSOE government, Spain elects the centre-right Partido Popular (PP).
2002	Peseta is replaced by euro as the official currency.
2004	Terrorist bombs on trains in Madrid kill 191 people and indirectly lead to a change of government, and the return to power of the Socialist party.
2006	The mayor of Marbella and several councillors are arrested for allegedly accepting bribes. Spain, Britain and Gibraltar agree to greater cooperation, including shared use of the airport.
2008	General election returns the Socialists to power.
2010	Spain goes into financial crisis after the property development boom comes to an end.
2013	New high-speed AVE train line to open between Madrid and Almería.

Moorish Spain

For centuries after the Reconquest of the Iberian peninsula by Christian armies, Andalucía felt ambivalent about the era that had done most to mark its landscapes, cities and culture – the six and a half centuries of rule by the Muslim peoples from North Africa known as the Moors. Christianity had proved its military superiority and did its best to belittle or destroy the civilisation it had conquered. But despite all the mosques that were converted into churches, Moorish Spain's greatest glories, both material and intangible, are today much more highly appreciated than they have been at any time over the last five centuries.

In the Andalucian countryside, the Moors laid an agricultural foundation without which much of the region would have remained scrubby desert. Without agriculture, neither the Moors nor their Christian successors could have fed, clothed or financed the villages and towns that in turn supported Seville and other cities. They were particularly adept at irrigation, and their ingenious watercourses can be seen here and there still gurgling around hillsides feeding terraced fields.

The Moors' most enduring contribution was urban and architectural. As well as the great palaces at Seville, Granada and Córdoba, they built lesser but no less exquisite monuments at Medina Azahara, Ronda, and the *alcazabas* (fortresses) at Almería and Málaga. Towns and villages all over Andalucía are bound by higgledy-piggledy street plans laid down by the Moors in which buildings blend into one another and sometimes fortification is indistinguishable from habitation.

In their buildings the Moors freely borrowed, adapted and improved on existing archaeological elements. The classical Moorish horseshoe arch for instance, as seen in the Mezquita at Córdoba, was taken from a pattern used in church design by the Visigoths. This was mixed with increasingly elaborate stucco work and the use of religious texts as decorative detail.

An expert eye can see the way Moorish architecture evolved, but there are always certain constant features to look out for: air, light, water and space. Running water acted as air conditioning, ionised and cleared air, and aided meditation.

Light was mediated through arched galleries and filigree screens such as the Almohad arches of the Patio del Yeso in the Alcázar. Space was kept in proportion but rarely stinted, as the Alhambra attests.

One of the Moors' less visible contributions to Spain was intellectual. Over the several centuries and eras of Moorish rule, they introduced medicine, mathematics, philosophy and law, among other disciplines. In the 12th century Córdoba alone produced the philosopher and physician Averroës (1126–88) and the Jewish philosopher, jurist and physician rabbi Moses ben Maimon, more commonly known as Maimonides (1135–1204), the 'father' of modern medicine.

As Christianity became the established orthodoxy, the last Moors were driven into obscurity in the hills and finally forced to convert or go into exile. Some chose to stay and live without their faith and their customs; others felt they had no choice but to leave.

The conquerors sought to eradicate or belittle their Islamic cultural legacy or to put their own stamp of authority on it, as can be seen in the cathedral placed in the middle of the mosque at Córdoba, or Charles V's Renaissance palace which stands awkwardly within the precinct of the Alhambra. The heritage of Andalucía, however, would be much less rich were it not for the part played by Spain's Muslims.

Moorish architecture – Córdoba's magnificent Mezquita

Politics

Any European country where, as recently as 1981, factions in the military thought they could overthrow the government by holding parliament hostage has to have an interesting political history.

The coup attempt of 23 February 1981, led by Colonel Antonio Tejero Molina, was both a test and a proof of Spain's brand-new (1977) democracy. Tejero and his men held the Cortes, or parliament, hostage for 24 hours before surrendering. Interestingly, the man responsible for the coup's failure was King Juan Carlos I, who had used Franco's death as an opportunity to usher in a new, modernising democracy. Tejero's rebels, controlled by shadowy figures higher up the armed forces hierarchy, claimed that Juan Carlos supported the coup. When the king informed the country's top generals that he opposed the rebellion, it fell apart.

While disturbing at the time, the attempted coup proved to most Spanish people that their young democracy was robust enough to withstand armed insurrection.

For centuries, a grotesque imbalance of wealth and power had undermined any attempts to stabilise Spanish politics. The advent of *latifundismo*, the distribution of great tracts of land to cronies after the Reconquest, only intensified the disparity, especially in Andalucía, which was the largest and most agricultural of all Spain's regions.

Even the 'Golden Age' of global conquest and trade did little more than enrich the already wealthy, and perhaps ease the emergence of a new, educated middle class. It took revolution and the industrialisation of northern Europe to suggest different models of politics.

Spain watched the French Revolution (1789–99) with interest. Spanish radicals attempted to establish a liberal constitution in Cádiz in 1812, only for it to be quashed by Fernando VII. It was the knock-on effect of industrialisation in northern Europe – negligible in Andalucía, but Barcelona's cotton trade rivalled Manchester's in the mid-19th century – that set in motion the forces that would transform Spain.

Social unrest began to spread across southern Spain in the mid-19th century, despite failed attempts at republican government. In 1923 General Primo de Rivera launched a military coup, and his junta ruled until 1930. In 1931 the Second Republic was established, prompting the far right to launch the Falange two years later. Increasing tensions between the two sides broke out into Civil War, with General Franco becoming head of state in 1936. Spain remained under his dictatorship until his death in 1975.

Under the constitution of 1978 which returned Spain to democracy, considerable power was devolved to the 17 *comunidades autónomas* (autonomous regions), Andalucía being the second largest of them. It is governed by the Junta de Andalucía, based in Seville, which has its own elected prime minister (*presidente*) and parliament. The region is subdivided into provinces and the provinces into *municipios* (towns), each under the jurisdiction of an *ayuntamiento* (town council) and its *alcalde* (mayor).

Unlike the Basques and Catalans in the north, Andalucians have a relatively weak sense of their collective identity, and the closest they have ever come to having an independence movement was during the Second Republic, immediately before the Civil War, when reformer Blas Infante (1885–1936) called for Andalucía to have more say over its own affairs – a demand that many people would say is largely met by the present system of devolution.

Ronda's Town Hall

Culture

Flamenco may be the most famous performance art form in Andalucía, but there's a lot more by way of entertainment and culture in the region. To begin with there is a rich calendar of traditional fiestas, many with their roots in pre-Christian times. As for contemporary art, the cities of southern Spain are on the major concert and exhibition circuits of Europe, and there is a growing sense of Andalucía promoting its own cultural heritage, particularly anything and everything to do with the Moors.

The cultural influence of Andalucía

This culture has produced or been adopted by numerous painters – not least Velázquez, Picasso, Zurbarán, Goya and Murillo – and writers – famously, poets Federico García Lorca, Luis Cernuda and Antonio Machado, and earlier figures such as Tirso de Molina (author of the original *Don Juan*) and peripatetic legend Cervantes. It has also been adopted by contemporary figures such as novelist Juan Goytisolo, and has attracted a lengthy queue of others ready to pledge their *afición* (fondness) for the region, not least Washington Irving and Prosper Mérimée (creator of Carmen).

Music and dance

As well as producing Cádiz's favourite musical son, Manuel de Falla, Andalucía also gave the world two legends of classical and flamenco guitar, Andrés Segovia and Paco de Lucía, not to mention dancers Cristina Hoyos and Joaquín Cortés.

The thriving university cities, most notably Seville itself, Granada and Cádiz, have generated an energetic youth culture, particularly since *la movida*, 'the movement', swept away the restrictions of the Franco era in the early 1980s. A vibrant underground music scene has spawned post-punk and electro bands that have been successful in Spain but are rarely heard of abroad. Perhaps uniquely across Europe, Andalucian nightclubs and concerts segue between contemporary dance culture and traditional flamenco and other indigenous folk and popular styles, with audiences displaying equal enthusiasm for both.

Perhaps because Andalucía sits at a junction between three continents, north African, eastern Mediterranean and Central/South American influences are often as recognisable as those from northern Europe or the United States in Spanish popular music. This mixture might best be heard in the work of cult 'world' music band Radio Tarifa. And again perhaps uniquely in European popular music, this is popular music sung in the band's own language.

The home of flamenco (*see pp18–19*) has long had an aversion to the North American invention, jazz, but in recent decades it has produced world-class jazz musicians. Of a newer generation, Chano Domínguez is just one Andalucian who has translated to the world circuit, and the contemporary flamenco giant Enrique Morente (*see p19*) makes frequent sorties into the world of jazz. Seville, Granada and Cádiz all have annual festivals that span many of the arts, and some hold specialist jazz or ethnic music festivals.

Fiestas

Every city, town and village has at least one traditional fiesta a year, invariably centring on some day of religious significance for the local *patrón* (patron saint) and involving rituals in the church and colourful processions through the streets. Every fiesta is, in effect, a celebration of local culture in its widest definition. The programme is likely to include folk dancing, arts events and other spectacles, with communal meals at which to sample local foods and wines. Easter Week (*see pp38–9*) is the busiest fiesta week in the calendar. Other important fiestas in Andalucía are listed on pages 20–21.

Seville's world-class Maestranza opera house

Culture

Flamenco

Flamenco, the archetypal Andalucian musical form that for many is the sound of Spain, has long been in dire need of demystifying, nowhere more so than in the matter of those castanets. These should be followed swiftly by the gaudy polka-dot gypsy dresses that Spanish women wear to dance the *sevillana*, in turn often mistaken as the 'authentic' flamenco dance.

All of the above 'customs' are almost wholly alien phenomena grafted on to flamenco in the 20th century, much to the anguish of some of flamenco's more traditionalist performers and aficionados.

Few histories of flamenco agree on its origin. Many concur that it took root among the East European Roma, or gypsy, population who arrived in Spain in the 18th century. Some go back further, to the 15th century and the transition of Arabic folk from the lute to the guitar. Others point to the fascinating recurrence of song forms, themes and instrumentation among folk musics around the Mediterranean littoral. Some even trace flamenco back to Roman times.

What all historians agree on, however, is how difficult it can be to hear the real thing today. Flamenco's seed-bed, the cafés, bars and clubs of 19th-century Seville and Jerez, gave way to a commercialised entertainment, the *tablao* (show, or tableau), at the turn of the 20th century. Even the once notorious flamenco caves of the gypsy Sacromonte area of Granada have become tourist attractions, with the result that the *gitanos* tend to keep their (usually ad hoc) celebrations to themselves and their friends. It requires a certain detective work, or at least reliable contacts, to locate bona fide flamenco today.

The fundament of flamenco is the vocal form known as *cante jondo* ('deep song'), originally and often today unaccompanied, apart from hand percussion. It is here that we locate the essence of flamenco, *duende* (meaning 'spirit'). Like swing, or the blues, *duende* is an unquantifiable spirituality glimpsed fleetingly during a performance of great passion, most commonly found at *gitano juergas*, private parties. The greatest *cantaor* (male singer) of the 20th century, El Camarón, died from excesses of drink and drugs aged 40 in 1992.

The distinctive flounces of flamenco dresses

Danzas or *bailes* (both meaning 'dances') soon began to accompany the *cante jondo*, as did regional variants such as the *fandango* from Cádiz and the *malagueña* from Málaga. Similarly, the *sevillana* was a medieval country dance appropriated by flamenco.

While traditionalists bemoan the commercialisation of flamenco, the spirit of *duende* has moved on, and probably into the hands of a performer such as Enrique Morente. Morente has pushed the envelope of flamenco more than anyone, producing flamenco Masses, working with improvising jazz groups, even delving into electronics and avant-garde sound with bands such as fellow Granadinos Largartija Nick.

Inevitably, flamenco has crossed over with rock and dance music, to the chagrin of purists. Yet to anyone who has observed the dissipation of other Mediterranean folk music traditions, such as Greek *syrtaki*, the success of bands such as Ketama and Radio Tarifa (both of which have now broken up) suggests that Spain's young are maintaining a powerful link with tradition that has simply been abandoned elsewhere.

Festivals and events

Most of the important events in the calendar of Andalucía are fiestas that are religious in origin, but there are also many arts festivals, often sponsored by regional or local government. Ferias (fairs) that began as livestock markets have since become grand social occasions, where the object is to dress up, to be with people, to see and be seen.

Easter, the biggest event of the year (*see pp38–9*), sets the date for Carnaval, which falls in February or March immediately before Lent, and for Whitsuntide (or Pentecost) and Corpus Christi (both of which fall between mid-May and mid-June). If you are thinking of attending one of the grand events of the Andalucian year, either book well in advance – hotels fill up at inflated prices – or stay somewhere not too far away where you can get the occasional rest from all the noise.

January

Fiesta de San Antón *16–17 January, Huescar.* Massive firework display with a celebration of local cuisine.
16–17 January, El Ejido, Almería. Processions culminate in a vast bonfire.

February

Carnaval Cádiz's Carnaval is the largest in mainland Spain, with parades and costumes. Most communities celebrate, although at a slightly more sedate pitch.

Flamenco viene del sur *February–May, Córdoba.* Shows in different venues around the city.

March–April

Semana Santa (Holy Week) *From late March to late April.* Almost everywhere in Andalucía celebrates Holy Thursday and Good Friday with solemnity and Easter Sunday with jubilation. Seville is famous for its processions, but they are also good in Granada and Málaga.
Feria de Abril (April Fair) *Late April.* Immediately after Holy Week, Seville stages a week-long party in flamenco dress in a showground across the river from the city centre.

May

Cruzes de Mayo *Early May, Córdoba.* Competition for the best floral decorations in the old town.
Feria de los Patios *First week in May, Córdoba.* The old town opens its domestic patios.

Feria del Caballo *Mid-May, Jerez de la Frontera.* Traders descend on the oldest country event and biggest animal fair in Andalucía.

Romería el Rocío *Whitsun week, El Rocío.* The most famous religious pilgrimage in Andalucía, in which up to half a million pilgrims converge on this small town to celebrate its miraculous icon of the Virgin.

May–June

Corpus Christi *May or June, Zahara de la Sierra.* Zahara celebrates by cladding the entire town centre in living greenery for just one day.

Romería de los Gitanos *Mid-June, Cabra.* Major *gitano* pilgrimage to the shrine of the Virgen de la Sierra.

Candelas de San Juan *23 June, Véjer de la Frontera.* Bonfires and a giant pyrotechnic bull illuminate this white village.

July

Festival Internacional de Música y Danza de la Cueva de Nerja Month-long festival of classical and popular concerts by world-class performers in the town's remarkable cave system.

Fiesta de la Virgen del Carmen *16 July, Marbella and elsewhere on the coast.* Images of the Virgin are carried in procession in decorated fishing boats.

August

Exaltación del Río Guadalquivir *Last two weekends in August, Sanlúcar de Barrameda.* Dramatic horse races, said

Seville's elegant Museo de Bellas Artes

to date back thousands of years, along a low-tide track on the beach, with landward celebrations in this town famed for its seafood and manzanilla sherry.

August–September

Ferias Towns across Andalucía celebrate colourful fairs, often staggered to allow towns to visit each other's festivities. Two of the biggest are in Granada and Málaga.

September

La Goyesca *First week in September, Ronda.* Ronda's autumn fair closes with the Goyesca bullfight, fought in the costumes shown in Goya's paintings of bullfighting scenes.

September–October

Wine Harvest Festivals (Vendimia) Andalucía's wine-producing towns celebrate the gathering of the grapes and the making of the year's wine. The biggest festival is in Jerez de la Frontera.

Impressions

It can take patience to get around and get things done in Andalucía, but slowing down to fit into the pace of local life is not necessarily a bad thing. The region has a good transport infrastructure, making it easy to travel about, and if you get lost people will be only too willing to point you in the right direction. Arriving in a new town by whatever means, invariably a good policy is to head for the plaza mayor (main square) and get your bearings. The tourist information office is likely to be close by.

When to go

Spring and autumn are usually the best times to visit Andalucía, although a run of El Niño summers has unbalanced the traditional pattern of clement springs and autumns, ferociously hot summers and temperate winters. It can be balmy in midwinter and unexpectedly rainy in high summer, although droughts are a regular occurrence throughout Andalucía.

Seville's *Semana Santa*, or Holy Week, and to a lesser extent the subsequent April Fair, require stamina, a plump wallet and military planning. Hotels book up as much as six months in advance, room prices can triple and some central hotels are so close to the round-the-clock celebrations that sleep is out of the question.

In August, many city people move to the beach so this is a relatively quiet time to go sightseeing in a city – if you can stand the heat.

Spring, which can begin as early as February, is the ideal time to visit although late autumn and even mid-winter can surprise with mild, sunny and even hot days – but be prepared for the rains that keep Andalucía so fertile. Layers of clothing for hot days and cool nights are best, and a light waterproof is always good insurance.

Getting around

If you stay in the cities and only make the occasional excursion to some well-known sight, you should find the public transport network perfectly adequate. Seville, Córdoba and Granada have compact city centres with some pedestrianised streets making walking the best way to get around. In labyrinthine quarters like Santa Cruz and the Albaicín, foot is the only sensible way to go and you may well get where you are going faster than the traffic. In fact, strolling (and even getting mildly lost, as long as you keep your wits about you and keep an eye out for landmarks) can be one of the pleasures of a visit. For more distant

The magnificent Plaza de España in Seville

sights you can extend your range by taking the occasional bus or taxi.

If you are on a tight schedule or you want to follow your nose to remote places and take your own time, you will need a car to get about.

Coach travel

All the major towns and cities of Andalucía are connected by bus (and sometimes by train as well) which can allow you to concentrate on the landscape, and people, rather than the road in front of you. Public transport is clean, safe and efficient. If you are just hopping between city centres you may as well use public transport in preference to hiring a car, and walk or take taxis as necessary. (*See pp182–3.*)

Seville has two main bus termini: at Plaza de Armas, near the Puente de Cachorro bridge on the banks of the Guadalquivir, and at Prado de San Sebastián on Avenida de Carlos V, a block away from the Jardines de Murillo. Plaza de Armas buses head west and north, San Sebastián buses south. Taxi drivers will often ask where you are going and head for the right bus station anyway.

Cycling

Cycling as a practical means of travel (as opposed to a sport) is still fairly uncommon in Andalucía, but an awareness of the health and environmental benefits of cycling is growing. The cities have some dedicated cycle lanes, most tourist resorts have bicycle hire facilities and in the countryside there are now *Vías Verdes* (green ways) using abandoned rail tracks as recreational routes. Cycle-touring, however, can be more stressful than rewarding as there are comparatively few minor roads and many are badly signposted. On main roads you should take particular care, as many drivers are completely unaware of the needs of cyclists.

Driving

Andalucía has a superb network of motorways linking its major cities and some good main roads too, but minor roads are variable and occasionally you'll find yourself on a bumpy back road that hasn't been repaired for decades.

If you are travelling by car, it's wise to avoid entering cities where parking is likely to be difficult. If you have to, plan ahead by choosing a hotel with a secure car park or finding out about multi-storey car parks near to where you want to go. It also makes sense not to drive into small villages because their narrow street patterns were never designed to allow cars to pass easily. Instead, park on the outskirts and walk in. Wherever you park your car, make sure you leave nothing visible at all inside it that may tempt someone to break in to see what else there is.

Although some drivers may flout the signs and lines of the highways, that doesn't mean there is no highway code, and the police can be quick to penalise errant motorists, often with on-the-spot fines. Speed limits, unless otherwise indicated, are 50kph (31mph) in built-up areas, 90kph (56mph) on roads outside towns and 120kph (75mph) on motorways. Beware of meeting a STOP sign where you might reasonably expect a 'Give Way', and of traffic lights following each other so that you go through a green light but are stopped immediately by a red one.

For more information on hiring cars and driving in Spain, *see p181*.

Taxis

Taxi drivers work to a meter and fixed charges for a list of destinations that drivers carry in their cab. There may be an extra charge per item of luggage in the boot. Premium fares kick in late at night and on festival days. Ask for an estimate – *¿Cuánto cuesta?* (How much?) – if unsure.

Trains

The Santa Justa rail station has links to Madrid and on to northern Europe, as well as regional destinations such as Cádiz, Córdoba, Granada, Huelva, Málaga and beyond (*see pp182–3*). The RENFE rail network is cheap, clean and usually efficient, although it doesn't reach all places in Andalucía. Where it does go, the train is a great way to see the country – the Bobadilla–Jimena de la Frontera route is generally regarded as one of the great mountain rail journeys of Europe. There are also some lesser-known services in Andalucía, such as the five-hour high-speed journey from Algeciras to Madrid, or the overnight hotel train to Barcelona that leaves Málaga each evening and arrives the following morning. RENFE has an excellent website with route maps, times and prices, online booking and an English-language edition at *www.renfe.es*. For full details, *see pp182–3*.

Banks and credit cards

Virtually all bank ATMs in Spain are international and will dispense euros against your home account, although not all banks will exchange foreign currency or traveller's cheques. Look for the *Cambio* (Change) sign, ideally with a neighbouring *sin comisión* (no commission) notice.

Credit cards (Amex, Diners, Visa, MasterCard etc) are widely accepted, although not always in smaller shops and restaurants.

Restaurants and bars

The Spanish eat late: lunch is rarely before 2pm, dinner anything between 9pm and midnight or later. Traditionally, lunch is the larger meal and dinner a light supper or tapas. Unless a bill stipulates otherwise, service is usually included, although it's considered polite to round up to the tidiest near figure. If you feel you've been well served or the food deserves special thanks, a tip of 10 per cent is sufficient.

Bars vary from tiny hole-in-the-wall kiosks to state-of-the-art designer cocktail joints. Food or a snack is considered an integral part of having a drink with friends, and many bars will serve a free tapa, unasked, with each drink. Most bars will also have a tapas menu with prices. Prices at the bar are often different (cheaper) than table service, and some outdoor bars and restaurants will also charge extra for terrace service. Tipping is discretionary, and less common than in restaurants.

Nightlife

The nocturnal behaviour of the Spanish can baffle even the long-term visitor. Especially in the summer months, they won't think of going out until it already seems late and they can often keep going – usually drinking very little – until well into the morning, or even until it is time to go to work. Few clubs open before 11pm or midnight, most only really warm up around 2am or later, and most hip nightclubs will tell you not to bother showing up until 4am. Most late-night bars are free, and many nightclubs offer free entry early in the night, with prices (normally covering a first drink) rising as the night proceeds. In some city centre areas, clubs may operate dress codes against jeans and trainers.

Women travellers

While circumstances have changed drastically for women travellers in Spain, certain precautions remain advisable, particularly for the lone traveller. While a younger, educated generation of males has been learning from its sisters, aunts and female contemporaries, women travelling without men are still considered a cultural anomaly in the depths of the Spanish countryside. The common-sense precautions for any city or town – avoiding unlit and sparsely populated areas, dressing to avoid snatch thieves, declining unwanted attention politely but firmly, looking as if you know where you're going and so on – apply here as anywhere. Unusually, women travelling with babies or small children can expect the VIP treatment: the Spanish adore children, and hotels and restaurants go out of their way to welcome them.

Gay and lesbian life

The *movida* (movement) of the post-Franco early 1980s triggered an avalanche of social changes, although largely in the cities. Women's rights, lesbian and gay rights and a whole raft of other emancipation movements were swept along by a wave of modernisation that had been held back since the 1960s.

The age of consent for gays and lesbians in Spain is 16, as across the EU. There are large lesbian and gay communities in Cádiz, Granada, Málaga, Seville and the beach resort of Torremolinos. There are often gender-specific bars and cafés, and nightclubs devoted to dress codes such as leather, but most are mixed and often quite popular with heterosexuals as well.

Law

If you happen to encounter, or need the assistance of, Spain's legal system it is best to note that it – or at least its public face – comes armed and isn't terribly friendly.

There are three distinct branches of law enforcement in Spain. The *Guardia Civil* wear combat-like green militaristic uniforms. Visitors will probably only encounter them

operating spot-checks on motorways. However, in some rural areas, these may be the only law officers on duty.

The *Policía Nacional* (PN), in their navy blue uniforms, can be thought of as the main urban police force and it is to one of their police stations (*comisarías*) you will need to go if you are in a city or holiday resort and you need to report a crime.

Some towns and cities have their own squads of *Policía Local* or *Municipal*, whose uniform colour varies from place to place. They carry out low-level policing duties such as dealing with drunks and towing away cars that have been badly parked. If an officer of the *Policía Local* can't assist with a

Tourist shops line the narrow streets in Seville

problem, he or she will usually know where to turn to for help.

Although each of these is armed, the PN heavily so, most visitors to Spain probably won't even notice them. There are some circumstances, however, where forewarned could be forearmed.

Identification: Everyone in Spain, visitors included, is expected to carry some means of identification. All Spanish citizens carry a DNI (National Identity Card). Normally, these are only used to verify ID against credit card transactions. In theory, if you are stopped by the police and don't have ID on you, you can be spot-fined or even arrested and jailed. Hotels will often keep passports briefly, to confirm identity, but should return them after verification.

Nude or topless bathing: Many resorts have designated nudist bathing beaches, and topless bathing is quite widespread on beaches in more developed resorts. Take local advice and be aware that what might be acceptable dress on the beach can cause offence away from it and in less sophisticated locales. The same applies to dressing to visit churches and other monuments.

Drugs: Spain's attitude to drugs has changed over the last few decades. During the 1980s there was a period of liberalisation and tolerance, but official attitudes have since hardened, largely as a consequence of crime and social problems related to drug abuse and addiction.

Because of the proximity of Andalucía to North Africa and the connections with South America, drugs are widely available but possession even of small amounts ('for personal use') is illegal. It is up to the police how far the law is enforced, and the best advice to the visitor is to proceed with caution and be well informed. The possession of softer drugs is punishable by a fine, but the use, and particularly trafficking, of harder drugs can incur a prison sentence.

Consulates and embassies

Most countries have consulates or representatives in Seville and Málaga, and embassies in Madrid, who will assist or advise with robberies, loss or theft of passports, emergency repatriation and so on. If arrested, you have the legal right to contact your consulate, although their willingness to become involved varies from country to country.

Insurance

For Britons and other EU citizens the European Health Insurance Card (EHIC) should smooth access to any necessary medical treatment in accident and emergency or outpatients' departments or at a medical centre. However, the advice to visitors from outside the EU – to take out a travel insurance policy with adequate health and repatriation cover – should also be taken seriously by EU residents. Some treatments and medications can only be obtained privately, and even under a health insurance scheme this will have to be paid for and claimed against the policy.

Seville

Seville leaps out on the unwary first-time visitor. Approached from any direction, by car, bus or train, its skyline starts to bristle with modernist bridgespans, church spires and half-glimpsed monuments such as the Plaza de Toros, the Torre del Oro and, of course, La Giralda tower.

Seville is remarkably compact. The city centre consists of four *barrios*, or districts: Santa Cruz, La Macarena, El Arenal and Parque de María Luisa. Most of the key sights are within walking distance of each other: the cathedral and La Giralda tower and Reales Alcázares palaces and gardens in Santa Cruz; the Plaza de España and the pavilions of the 1929 Exposition.

The city is a palimpsest of different historical eras and styles, as over the centuries layers of different cultures – Roman, Visigoth, Berber, Almohad, Mudéjar, Gothic, Renaissance, Baroque and, across the Río Guadalquivir, the alarming perspectives and colour-schemes of 20th-century post-modernism around the Expo 92 site – were imposed on each other.

ORIENTATION

The natural place to get your bearings in Seville is in the Plaza del Triunfo. Standing facing the cathedral, with La Giralda tower looming above you, you have the other major sight of Seville, the Reales Alcázares, directly behind you. To your right (eastwards) are the dense streets of Santa Cruz, the most picturesque part of the city.

Going to your left a few steps takes you past the Archivo de Indias on to the broad Avenida de la Constitución. Turn right up this street and cross the square in front of the city hall, and you will reach the main shopping district of the city around Calle de las Sierpes. Keep going in this direction, northwards, and you will be in La Macarena quarter where there are only a few scattered sights to see.

Turning left down Constitución instead takes you towards the Parque de María Luisa and the magnificent Plaza de España. Before you get there you'll pass the university, formerly the tobacco factory of Carmen fame.

Across Avenida de la Constitución from the Plaza del Triunfo, meanwhile, is the old harbourside quarter of El Arenal that stretches down to the banks

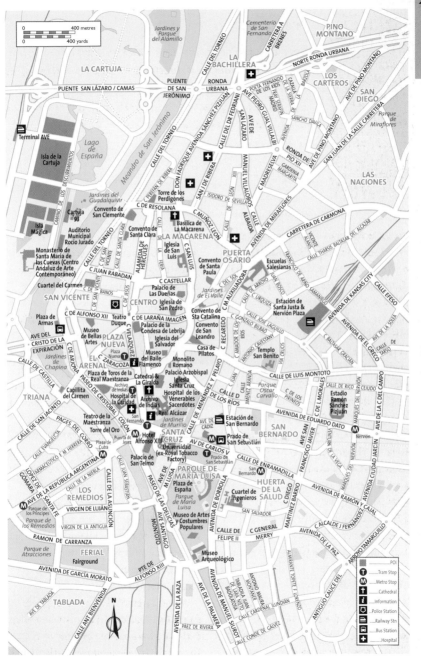

Parque de María Luisa

of the Guadalquivir. Its main sights, the Torre del Oro and bullring, are on the riverbank itself. Two bridges lead from here into the Triana district on the other side of the river.

Lifestyle

The enduring appeal of Seville lies as much in the lifestyle led by its people on its streets as in the grandeur of the historic monuments that loom above them. The mythology insists that, among all the Spanish peoples, the Andalucians are both the most passionate and the most laid-back.

Fun of the Fair

Spring, and April in particular, are the best times to visit Seville if you like life at its most intense or the times to avoid if you want to see the city in its more normal mood. In this period of the year Seville holds large celebrations of contrasting character. The first is *Semana Santa* (Holy Week), leading up to Easter Sunday, when *nazarenos*

(penitents) in the pointed hoods and robes of the Inquisition march through the neighbourhoods day and night. Onlookers are often moved to strong emotions and some spontaneously burst into song.

After a short breather of a week or so, the Sevillanos then plunge into their beloved *Feria de Abril*, the April Fair. This takes place in a purpose-built fairground across the river from the city centre. Just follow the flow of people – the women in flouncy flamenco dresses – and you'll find it. In essence it is an amalgam of private parties taking place in enclosures called *casetas*, but you are free to wonder the streets of the fairground people-watching and soaking in the hedonistic atmosphere of a city dressed to the nines but with its hair down.

A working city

Like other Andalucian cities, Seville lives partly on the direct and indirect revenues derived from tourism, but it is more than a fossilised historical theme park; it is also a working city. As capital of Andalucía, it is a political, administrative and service centre for southern Spain. It also has a large university that helps stimulate a whole sector of the economy dedicated to culture: concert halls, bookshops, theatres and so on.

Street culture

It is also a city where you will find yourself thrown into the culture as soon as you step outside: unless you hide in your hotel, you will find yourself having breakfast, lunch and dinner elbow-to-elbow with the Sevillanos. Indeed, despite those periods when Atlantic weather systems push up the Guadalquivir valley to drench Seville, much of life is conducted out of doors, even in winter, when the bars of Santa Cruz, Triana and La Macarena deploy pavement heaters to warm their patrons. In the outdoor bars around calles Mateos Gago and Rodrigo Caro in Santa Cruz, it is possible to plunge into the street culture of Seville in the shadow of its two greatest cultural monuments: La Giralda tower and the façades of both the cathedral and the Reales Alcázares.

Exploring Andalucía

Although Seville is in the extreme west of Andalucía, it still forms a good base for excursions around the region. It is at the hub of an extremely good motorway network and there are trains to all of the other major towns and cities. Córdoba, Jerez de la Frontera (famous for sherry) and Doñana National Park can be visited on day trips from the city. Granada, Ronda, Málaga and the white towns of Cádiz are not much further away: they could be done in a day each, but are more rewarding with an overnight stay.

SANTA CRUZ

The former Jewish quarter is the liveliest and most historically charged of all Seville's *barrios*. As well as the Reales Alcázares and the cathedral (*see pp32, 34–5, 36–7*), it also encompasses the Archivo de Indias, the 16th-century repository of documents relating to Spain's conquest of meso-America, the exquisite 17th-century Hospital de los Venerables Sacerdotes, the Jardines de Murillo and the Palacio de la Condesa de Lebrija.

Of equal interest is the life of this busy *barrio*. Starting on Calle Mateos Gagos, leading off the northeast corner of the Plaza del Triunfo, Santa Cruz's scrambled streets and alleys conceal some of Seville's finest bars and restaurants, and some of its best hotels. Most nights of the week and most weeks of the year, its bars and restaurants are thronged with Sevillanos and visitors who have stumbled on this carelessly kept secret.

Alcázar

Andalucians and visitors alike are split over the charms of Seville's Alcázar (fortress) compared to those of its nearest rival, Granada's Alhambra and Generalife gardens. The Alcázar is smaller and more enclosed than the rambling open-air Alhambra, which perhaps gives its courtyards, halls and spectacular décor an intensity lacking in Granada's hilltop monument.

There has been a structure on the site of the Alcázar since Roman times, and palatial accommodation for royalty since the 14th century. It became a fort for the Córdoban caliphate in the 10th century and was expanded by Almohad rulers in the 12th century. Following the reconquest of Seville, King Pedro I, known as Pedro the Cruel to history but Pedro the Just to his cronies, began a programme of expansion that continued sporadically over the centuries.

Jardines del Alcázar

The gardens beyond were originally laid out in the 12th century but are today seen in 16th-century form. The gardens, a symmetrical jungle of towering palms and pines criss-crossed by watercourses and studded with fountains, have to be the most placid spot in the whole of Seville.
Tel: 954 50 23 23. www.patronato-alcazarsevilla.es. Open: winter daily 9.30am–5pm; summer daily 9.30am–7pm. Admission charge.

Palacio de Pedro I

The upper levels of the Palacio remain the property of the Spanish monarchy

Gardens designed for intrigues

Central Seville (*see pp44–5 for walk route*)

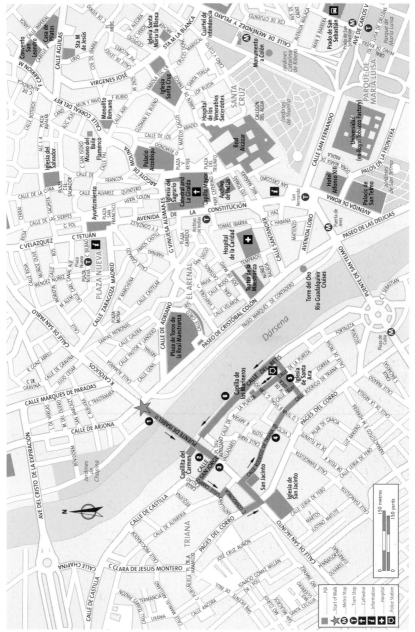

even today: King Juan Carlos I has apartments here, where his daughter Elena was married in 1995.

At the heart of the Palacio sits **Patio de las Doncellas**, the Patio of the Maidens, whose galleried upper floor gives on to a variety of private salons built at various stages in the Palacio's history. Here, in the minutely detailed plasterwork originally fashioned by hand by craftsmen from Granada, the visitor can take a measure of the extraordinary efforts that went into constructing this perfect space intended for the eyes of only a select few. The work that created this perfect symmetry would have taken years.

This effect increases in the neighbouring **Patio de las Muñecas**, the Patio of the Dolls (after two small faces to be found in one of its arches), where the arithmetical repetitions of

The elegant Patio del Yeso at the heart of the Alcázar

pattern are enhanced by the strong use of *azulejos* (glazed tiling) on the walls. This in turn leads on to the Alcázar's crowning glory, the **Salón de Embajadores**, the 15th-century Ambassadors' Hall, whose stunning domed ceiling, made of interlocking pieces of gilded wood, still dazzles today. It is a masterpiece of design from a culture where representational art was strictly forbidden (*see pp12–13*).

Patio del León

The Puerta del León, the entrance to the Alcázar, leads through original Almohad walls to the Patio del León courtyard, where Pedro dispensed summary justice after deliberating in the neighbouring Sala de la Justicia. Just off the Sala is the exquisite **Patio del Yeso**, a small multi-arched water garden with Almohad designs dating from the 12th century.

Patio de la Montería

This larger open-air patio, where the court would gather before hunting expeditions, is dominated by the entrance to the Palacio de Pedro I, which gives a hint of the architectural glories to come. The multilevelled balconied façade is a prime example of the rhythmic patterning of Mudéjar architecture.

Salones de Carlos V

The Salones de Carlos V were remodelled in the 16th century within an original 13th-century Gothic palace and today house a collection of historic tapestries hung beneath a magnificent vaulted ceiling.

Archivo de Indias

At the 'bottom' of the Plaza del Triunfo, this was originally built as a stock exchange to conduct Seville's crucial role as 'office' of the Spanish Americas. In 1785 it was converted into an archive dedicated to collecting documents relating to the colonial enterprise, and is nowadays said to house over 80 million pages of documents, most only available to scholars.
Plaza del Triunfo. Tel: 954 50 05 28.
Open: winter Mon–Fri 8am–3pm;
summer Mon–Fri 8am–2.30pm.
Free admission.

Callejón del Agua

No visit to Santa Cruz would be complete without a walk along the pedestrianised Callejón del Agua, a narrow alley running beneath the Alcázar garden walls and into the heart of the *barrio*.

Casa de Pilatos

This house was built in the 16th century by the first Marquess of Tarifa as a palatial storeroom for the artworks he gathered on his journeys around Europe and to the Holy Land. Subsequent occupants maintained the tradition and today the Casa rivals the Alcázar in its architectural splendour and the treasures it contains.

Columbus monument, Jardines de Murillo

Plaza Pilatos. Tel: 954 22 52 98.
www.fundacionmedinaceli.org.
Open: winter daily 9am–6pm; summer
daily 9am–7pm. Admission charge.

Hospital de los Venerables Sacerdotes

A former retirement home for 'venerable' priests, now used for exhibitions. It houses a splendid Baroque church.
Plaza de los Venerables.
Tel: 954 56 26 96. www.focus.abengoa.es.
Open: daily 10am–2pm & 4–8pm.
Guided tours only. Admission charge.

Jardines de Murillo

Plaza Santa Cruz, one of the oldest (1692) and prettiest of the *barrio*'s squares, gives on to these slender public gardens, named after the painter Bartolomé Murillo (1618–82) who lived in nearby Calle Santa Teresa, where his former house is now a museum.
The gardens feature a towering monument to Columbus.
Gardens open: sunrise–sunset.
Museo de Murillo, Calle Santa Teresa.
Tel: 955 03 72 63. Closed for restoration until summer 2011.

Museo del Baile Flamenco

A new museum in an 18th-century building, presenting flamenco dance in all its forms from its origins to the present day. There's also a programme of flamenco performances.
Calle Manuel Rojas Marcos 3
(near Plaza Alfalfa). Tel: 954 34 03 11.
www.museoflamenco.com.
Open: Mon–Fri 9.30am–7pm.
Admission charge.

Palacio de la Condesa de Lebrija

Around a hundred years ago the passion for all things archaeological, historical and artistic of Doña Regla Manjón Mergelina, Countess of Lebrija, led her to fill her 16th-century ancestral home with any and every object of beauty she could acquire. The result is an eclectic collection housed in an urban mansion, worth seeing in its own right. Many of the pieces – including splendid mosaics – came from the Roman remains at Italica. Among the other exhibits are Moorish pieces, tiles retrieved from a ruined convent and a Renaissance frieze.
Calle Cuna 8. Tel: 954 21 81 83.
www.palaciodelebrija.com. Open: winter Mon–Fri 10.30am–7.30pm, Sat 10am–2pm & 4–6pm, Sun 10am–2pm; summer Mon–Fri 9am–3pm, Sat 10am–2pm. Admission charge.

Catedral and La Giralda

Seville's cathedral and great bell tower, La Giralda, sit on the site of a mosque built by Almohad invaders who reached the city in 1147 and set about building the tower and the riverside Torre del Oro. When the Christians took Seville back in 1428, they converted the mosque into a Christian church and began the first of a series of alterations to the tower, starting with its Moorish dome and pinnacle. Today, the Moorish base is capped by a Renaissance belfry housing its fearsome carillon and topped by La Giralda weathervane, the figure of Faith astride the globe.

The mosque-church was demolished at the start of the 15th century in favour of a brand-new cathedral to accompany the tower. It took over a hundred years to build and when completed was said to be the largest Gothic church in the world. More recent calculations of its floor plan and volume suggest that it is indeed the largest Gothic church in the world and also contains the biggest altarpiece in the Christian world. It amply displayed the wealth of the city.

Capilla Mayor

The most remarkable feature of this church crammed with marvels is the Capilla Mayor, or main chapel, dominated by a vast *retablo* (altarpiece) featuring 45 scenes from the life of Christ. As befits the biggest cathedral on the planet, this is also the planet's biggest altarpiece, the life-work of one artist, Pierre Dancart.

La Giralda

The Giralda tower underwent no fewer than four major changes in design in the first 400 years of its existence, finally reaching the shape we see today in 1568. The ascent is not as frightening as it looks. La Giralda was built so that two mounted guards could patrol as far up as its belfry. As both men and their mounts needed a shallow gradient, a set of wide and gentle stairs spirals up towards the belfry, which affords magnificent 360-degree views out across the city.

Iglesia del Sagrario

This smaller church to the left of the entrance to the nave dates from the 17th century and is nowadays used as a parish church serving the local community.

Patio de los Naranjos

The Iglesia del Sagrario opens out into a curiosity in a Christian church: the Patio de los Naranjos, a handsome large courtyard lined with symmetrically planted orange trees. The space dates from the site's period as a mosque, and is where Moorish worshippers would have washed hands and feet in the central fountain before entering.

Tomb of Columbus

To the right of the vast Capilla Mayor is a small chapel containing the tomb installed in 1890 to house the remains of Columbus, which had been transported here from Cuba. His coffin is supported by four carved figures representing the royal houses of Castille, León, Aragón and Navarra.

Sacristía Mayor

Beyond the tomb, the Sacristía Mayor contains a collection of paintings by Murillo, and a sizeable collection of still more jewelled and gold-bound religious artefacts.

Catedral & La Giralda open: Mon–Sat 11am–5pm, Sun 2.30–6pm. Times may vary. Tel: 954 21 49 71 for details. Admission charge.

EL ARENAL

This historic *barrio,* between the Avenida de la Constitución and the Río Guadalquivir, is one of the oldest areas of the city. Before the river began to silt up in the 16th century, making it impossible for seagoing craft to reach

(Cont. on p40)

Semana Santa

No one forgets their first encounter with a *nazareno*, one of the hooded and cloaked penitents who form the processions that fill the streets of Seville and every other Spanish city and town during Easter. Accompanied by brass bands and lavishly decorated *pasos* (biers), carrying statues of the Virgin Mary and scenes from the Passion, the figures in their Klan-like disguises can strike terror in the unwitting spectator, and need some explaining.

The marches by local *hermandades* or *cofradías* (brotherhoods) date back as far as the 14th century and the

Barefoot penitents gather for a procession

Reconquest. The form they take today dates from the 17th century, when many of the sumptuous, larger-than-life statues of the Virgin and scenes from Christ's last days (roughly from Gethsemane to Golgotha) were first fashioned. The costumes, which were indeed copied by the USA's Ku Klux Klan for their scare factor, actually come from the anonymous robes of the Spanish Inquisition. At night, lit by braziers, the sight of the *nazarenos* weighed down in their panoply and accompanied by barefoot penitents in chains and rags dragging life-sized crosses behind them can resemble a tableau from a Gothic horror film. Yet these are largely seen as neighbourhood get-togethers and involve women as well as men, young people and even children. Membership of a *hermandad* is a much sought-after privilege, even by those who wouldn't normally see the inside of a church at any other time of the year.

The routes taken by the *pasos* weave through the streets from each *hermandad*'s local church towards the cathedral, and the further away the church – such as the Basilica de la Macarena – the longer the march:

Nazarenos (hooded and cloaked penitents) in one of Seville's solemn Easter marches

some can be on the streets for up to 12 hours. The biers can be heavy: depending on their size they can require anything between 40 and 90 bearers, working in relays and swaying in rhythm to displace the weight of the bier. The biers, *nazarenos* and community brass bands are interspersed with groups of local dignitaries and led by a *capataz*, or captain, who rings a bell to announce regular rest breaks, or sometimes just to let stragglers catch up.

Despite the solemn nature of the marches and the events for which they are atoning, the mood on the pavements is usually celebratory, especially so on Good Friday morning (Thursday from midnight, in fact), which is the climax of the week. (Processions continue until Easter Sunday, although these are less spectacular and thinly attended.) The Thursday daytime processions are sombre affairs, where visitors are asked not to dress in shorts and T-shirts out of respect, but otherwise the atmosphere is one of a long street party. The crowning moment is normally the arrival of La Macarena at the cathedral, usually around 6am on Friday, when even an atheist might feel moved by the Virgin, resplendent in her jewelled gowns and carried aloft on a bier decked with flowers and ablaze with candlelight.

While few other *Semana Santa* celebrations approach the intensity of those in Seville, almost every town and village will have its processions with the statue of the local Virgin Mary and scenes from the Passion. Tourist offices and local newspapers publish timetables and routes for each *hermandad*'s processions through the week.

Seville by the early 17th century, the site of El Arenal was the city's port and the hub of Spain's maritime commerce with the rest of the world. Both Columbus and Magellan sailed from here. El Arenal's maritime importance stretches further back, however, to the 12th-century Almohad invasion, when the Moors initiated the construction of both La Giralda tower and the Torre del Oro.

Hospital de la Caridad

El Arenal is inadvertently responsible for producing a quasi-mythic figure who himself inspired operas and drama, Don Juan. The 17th-century playboy-turned-philanthropist Miguel de Mañara is wrongly claimed by some to be the model for notorious seducer Don Juan Tenorio. Yet it was de Mañara who founded the charitable Hospital de la Caridad, still in use today to care for the elderly and infirm. Its chapel contains a small but vibrant collection of paintings by Murillo, Leal and others.

Calle Temprado 3. Tel: 954 22 32 32. Open: Mon–Sat 9am–1.30pm & 3.30–7.30pm, Sun 9am–1pm. Admission charge; free on Sunday.

Museo de Bellas Artes

This secular masterpiece lies at the northernmost edge of El Arenal. A former convent, the building now

View over the city from La Giralda tower

houses one of the finest collections of Spanish art under one roof, ranging from medieval to 20th-century but concentrating on the heyday of the 'Seville School' from the 15th century, in particular the works of Murillo, Zurbarán and Leal. The 16th-century convent building, built around three beautiful courtyards and crammed with interior details such as the domed ceiling of its Baroque gallery, is worth a visit in itself.

Plaza del Museo. Tel: 954 78 64 91. Open: Tue 2.30–8.30pm, Wed–Sat 9am–8.30pm, Sun 9am–2.30pm. Admission charge; free to EU citizens.

Plaza de Toros de la Real Maestranza

Seville's bullring is the oldest and most famous in the world. It was built in 1761 and is not so much a circle as a polygon of 30 sides, with a white and ochre Baroque façade. If you can't or don't want to attend a bullfight, you can always take a 20-minute tour of the bullring which takes in not only the arena, but also all the ancillary facilities, including the infirmary and chapel.

Paseo de Cristóbal Colón. Tel: 954 22 45 77. www.realmaestranza.com. Open: winter daily 9.30am–7pm; summer daily 9.30am–8pm. Admission charge.

Río Guadalquivir cruises

You'll get a different view of the city from the river. Cruceros Torre del Oro run one-hour trips every 30 minutes from 11am to 11pm, leaving from the wharf on Alcalde Marqués de Contadero, next to the Torre del Oro. In summer, there are cruises all the way down the river to its mouth at Sanlúcar de Barrameda and Doñana National Park. There is commentary in five languages.

For more information, tel: 954 56 16 92. www.crucerostorredeloro.com

Torre del Oro

This tower was originally a watchtower built into the defensive walls that surrounded the Alcázar and the city centre. It was taken back in the Reconquest less than a hundred years later, and in the 15th century the tower was used to store bounty brought back from the Americas. Today, it houses a modest maritime museum.

Paseo de Cristóbal Colón. Tel: 954 22 24 19. Open: Sept–Jul Tue–Fri 10am–2pm, Sat & Sun 11am–2pm. Admission charge.

BEYOND THE CENTRE

Santa Cruz and El Arenal will certainly be the main claims on your time in Seville, and if you only have a day or two there is no question of where you should spend them. But there are more things to see within a short walking distance to the north into La Macarena district, west to the river and across it (Triana and the former Expo site of Isla de la Cartuja), and especially south into the leafy Parque de María Luisa. If you prefer to save your legs, hop-on/hop-off tour buses will take you past everywhere worth seeing without you having to leave your seat.

Basílica de La Macarena

Heading northwards, Santa Cruz merges into the un-gentrified quarter of La Macarena, which has several interesting, rarely visited churches. The Baroque Basílica de La Macarena, next to some remains of the city's Arab walls, is where the much venerated statue of the Virgen de La Macarena is kept in a position of honour. This 17th-century statuette of the Virgin Mary with tears on her face in grief for her son draws a daily crowd of the faithful who come to make offerings

Icon of La Macarena

and beg her intercession in their problems. It is ceremoniously brought out of the church by the brotherhood that cares for it during Seville's Easter Week celebrations.

Calle Bécquer 1. Tel: 954 90 18 00.
Open: Mon–Sat 9am–2pm & 5–9pm,
Sun 9.30am–2pm & 5–9pm.
Free admission.

Isla de la Cartuja

Between April and October 1992, an estimated 36 million people visited the Expo 92 world fair that was held on the Isla de la Cartuja across the Guadalquivir from the centre of Seville. Judged an unqualified success in spite of the expense, Expo turned Seville into a modern city and put it (and Andalucía in general) much higher up the list of must-see destinations than it had previously been. However, the city has never figured out quite what to do with the Expo site (not an island despite its name). Strangely, considering the flagship event that took place there not so long ago, it is easy to visit Seville and not go near the Cartuja.

But there is charm in exploring what is in effect a postmodern archaeological site. Although many buildings stand empty and crumbling, and car parks have become covered by weeds, with the once cutting-edge cable car across the river standing forlorn, several of the Expo's innovative pavilions are still there to admire, many of them forming part of a technological business park. Note, however, that the lack of signposting can make it difficult to find your way around on foot so it might be a good time to sit on the upper deck of a tour bus and have the various pavilions and other Expo leftovers pointed out to you.

Isla Mágica

It's rare to find a theme park in an urban area, but this one around Expo 92's lake is only a short walk across the Puente de la Barquera bridge (a striking bit of architecture in itself) from La Macarena. It means that you don't have to go out of your way to visit it, and can incorporate it into a day of sightseeing. The forty rides are divided into eight zones.

Tel: 902 16 17 16 (information and reservations). www.islamagica.es. Opening times vary greatly throughout the year – check before visiting. Admission charge.

Monasterio de Santa María de las Cuevas (Centro Andaluz de Arte Contemporáneo)

If any building could be said to be suffering from schizophrenia, this is it. Built as a Carthusian monastery (after which the Isla de la Cartuja is named) in the 19th century, it was turned into a ceramics factory by a Liverpudlian entrepreneur. In 1992 it briefly served as the centrepiece for Expo, the only old building on the site. Its latest and

Some of La Cartuja's elaborate tile work

least interesting incarnation is as a gallery of contemporary art. You can regard the paintings as a bonus, however, as you stroll around the complex admiring the tiled decorations, the patio beside the church and the great ombú tree in the grounds, which is said to have been planted by Christopher Columbus's son Hernando.

Avenida Américo Vespucio 2. Tel: 955 03 70 70. www.caac.es. Open: Tue–Fri 10am–8pm, Sat 11am–8pm (closes 9pm in summer), Sun 10am–3pm. Admission charge, but free on Tue to EU citizens. Grounds free all the time.

Walk: Triana

A walk through the historic barrio *of Triana across the river from El Arenal is more about capturing the spirit of a place than visiting great monuments. For centuries, Triana was the* gitano *(gypsy) barrio, the mythic birthplace of flamenco, and also, coincidentally, the city's pottery district, a craft maintained to this day in its numerous* azulejo *(tiling) workshops.* See p33 for map.

Allow 2 hours.

Start at Puente de Isabel II.

1 Puente de Isabel II

Built of iron in 1852, it is one of nine bridges across the river and affords good views of the Guadalquivir. The river was the watery trade route on which Seville's wealth was based, from Roman times through the colonisation of the New World. The port of Seville, however, now deals more with pleasure boats and cruise ships than commercial traffic.

2 Capillita del Carmen

On the Triana side of the Puente de Isabel II is this curious *azulejo*-clad structure, a miniature chapel built in

The Puente de Isabel II, or Triana Bridge

1926. Directly opposite the Capillita is the distinctive yellow tower of El Faro de Triana, a bar-restaurant whose terraces give great views over the river.

3 Calle San Jorge
Take Calle San Jorge on the right to plunge into the pottery district. The most famous pottery workshop is **Cerámica Santa Ana** (*San Jorge 31*). Ceramics have been made in Triana since at least 1314 but the industry probably dates from earlier times than that. The Romans made amphorae here to fill with wine and oil. In Moorish times, Triana's workshops made ceramic tiles in blue, white and green. Before continuing, note the name of the small street off Calle Callao, Callejón de la Inquisición, a reminder of one of the first homes of the notorious investigators of heresy.
Turn left off Calle San Jorge into Calle Campos and continue along Calle Covadonga, passing more pottery shops. Turning left on to Pages del Corro and then left at Calle de San Jacinto, Triana's main thoroughfare, you find Calle Rodrigo de Triana on the first right.

4 Calle Rodrigo de Triana
Named after the sailor who first sighted the New World on Columbus's first trip in 1492, Rodrigo is a typical Triana street, with a view of your next destination, the Iglesia de Santa Ana, above its rooftops.

5 Iglesia de Santa Ana
The dense warren of streets between Calle de San Jacinto and the church is where Triana's displaced Roma population lived around communal courtyards, particularly on Calle Pelay Correa. The church was founded in the 13th century and is said to be the oldest parish church in Seville.
From the church, walk east towards the river. Either take Calle de la Pureza northwards towards the tiny Capilla de los Marineros, the 18th-century sailors' chapel, or continue to the riverfront and walk north along Calle Betis back towards the Puente de Isabel II.

6 Calle Betis
For many people, Calle Betis is the best part of Triana. It can seem like one long line of bars and restaurants pumping out *sevillana* flamenco music. Several of them have tables set on the riverbank, with a few, such as the famous Kiosco de las Flores, in private gardens. All the way there are relaxing views across the water of the bullring and the Torre del Oro, and you can watch canoeists, cruise boats and other river traffic come and go.
You can get back to El Arenal and Santa Cruz the way you came, but an alternative route is to turn right on Calle Betis to Plaza de Cuba. From here you can cross the Puente de San Telmo and either turn right into Parque de María Luisa or get back to Santa Cruz via the Puerta de Jerez.

Parque de María Luisa and the Plaza de España

In 1929 Seville staged the Ibero-American exhibition, a sort of Hispanic world fair that might have been a success if it hadn't taken place in the same year as the Wall Street Crash. However, the city was left with a beautiful park, the Parque de María Luisa, which has a prodigious collection of architecture scattered around it, all of which has been put to good use. Two pavilions, for instance, form museums of archaeology and of folk arts and crafts. The city's finest hotel, the Alfonso XIII, is also a legacy of the

Ceramics in the Plaza de España

exhibition. Even if you are not staying there you can go in for a meal or a drink, or simply to escape the noise of traffic for a while.

The most imposing monument in the park is the **Plaza de España**, a semicircle of arcades ending in two neo-Baroque towers. It is decorated with glorious ceramics and has a fountain and colourful benches depicting the provinces of Spain in alphabetical order.

Universidad (ex-Royal Tobacco Factory)

What is now part of Seville University was once Europe's biggest cigarette factory. It was here that Prosper Mérimée's fictional fiery heroine Carmen worked, rolling tobacco while she wasn't enflaming men's murderous passions. Bizet took the story and made it the basis of what is perhaps the world's most famous opera.

AROUND SEVILLE

It was only natural that, following the conquest of the Americas, Seville's wealth should spill over into the surrounding towns and villages. Seville's eastern flank, towards Córdoba, boasts some of the most beautiful towns in this part of Andalucía.

Carmona

Its proximity to Seville, combined with a wealth of architectural features and a number of excellent hotels,

makes this an ideal alternative to staying in Seville. With a regular (hourly) bus service (40 mins) into the centre of Seville, it's also an attractive option for drivers nervous of the capital's streets and reputation for car crime. At the heart of its warren of medieval streets is a lovely square, the Plaza de San Francisco.

Carmona has been inhabited since pre-Christian Iberian times. Following the Reconquest, it became a country residence for King Pedro I (Pedro the Cruel), architect of parts of the Reales Alcázares and the castle that is now Carmona's *parador* (part of a chain of luxury, state-run hotels). The Roman presence is preserved today, if only in the fascinating Necrópolis and vestigial auditorium on the outskirts. The town museum and several churches, including San Pedro, with a tower copied from La Giralda, record later architectural and cultural details.

Museo de la Ciudad

Housed in an 18th-century mansion, the town museum has a good collection of artefacts from key eras in the history of the town: prehistoric, Iberian, Roman, Moorish and Christian, including pieces from the Necrópolis.
Calle San Ildefonso. Tel: 954 14 01 28. Open: summer Mon 10am–2pm, Tue–Fri 10am–2pm & 6.30–8.30pm, Sat & Sun 9.30am–2pm; winter Mon 11am–2pm, Tue–Sun 11am–7pm. Admission charge.

Necrópolis Romana

Discovered in 1868, this partially excavated Roman burial site has so far revealed a handful of family tombs, communal crematoria and ossuaries, a villa-like tomb for the daughter of a local ruler and a mausoleum-temple dedicated to the worship of Cybele and Attis. Guided tours (30 mins) every 20 minutes.

Avenida Jorge Bónsor. Tel: 955 62 46 15. Open: summer Tue–Fri 9.30am–6pm, Sat & Sun 9.30am–3.30pm. Admission charge, but free to EU citizens.

Écija

Possibly the hottest town in Spain, at the heart of an area known as *la sartén* (the frying pan), Écija is an architectural oddity. A total of 11 15th- and 16th-century church towers dominate its old town centre, a measure, along with its impressive mansions, of Écija's wealth during the Golden Age and its position at the centre of the olive oil industry. The churches and towers are currently in various states of disrepair, and the town's history can be traced in the

Carmona's Puerta de Sevilla

The Antigua Universidad of Osuna

Museo Histórico Municipal.

Museo Histórico Municipal, Palacio de Benamejí, Calle Cánovas del Castillo 4. Tel: 955 90 29 19. Open: Oct–May Tue–Fri 10am–1.30pm & 4.30–6.30pm, Sat 10am–2pm & 5.30–8pm, Sun 10am–3pm; Jun–Sept Tue–Fri 10am–2.30pm, Sat 10am–2pm & 8–10pm, Sun 10am–3pm. Free admission.

Osuna

Built on a small mount in the plains east of Seville, Osuna is another cluster of fine Renaissance mansions topped by a trio of remarkable religious buildings. The lively Plaza Mayor and neighbouring Calle San Pedro are the best places to see the (private) mansions, most accessibly the Palacio de los Marquesas de la Gomera, now a five-star hotel. Clustered above the town are the Colegiata de Santa María, the Convento de la Encarnación and the Antigua Universidad.

Situated on the hill above the town. Colegiata and Convento open: Oct–Apr Tue–Sun 10am–1.30pm & 3.30–6.30pm; May–Sept Tue–Sun 10am–1.30pm & 4–7pm. Admission charge.

Old and new faces

Andalucía is one of the most ethnically diverse regions of Europe and becoming ever more so. Even before recorded history it was receiving waves of settlers and invaders. The Phoenicians, Carthaginians and Romans mixed with the indigenous prehistoric farming populations they found. The Moors came in successive migrations from North Africa beginning in the 8th century and similarly left their trace in the gene pool.

At some uncertain point of the Middle Ages, and from no precise origin, the gypsies (*gitanos*) arrived. They now form the region's largest ethnic minority, a community 300,000 strong. In general and with significant exceptions, the gypies are only semi-integrated into society and remain defiantly proud of their own traditions. Their contribution to Andalucian culture is evident in music and dance.

More recently, Andalucía has become a magnet for people converging on it literally from all four points of the compass.

As Spain's economy steadily improved after the reintroduction of democracy in the late 1970s, the country became a prize worth the effort for poor illegal immigrants from North Africa and sub-Saharan countries. Desperate people still come from these places, often paying exorbitant sums to middlemen to get them across the Strait of Gibraltar in small craft headed at night for beaches that cater for tourists during the day. The lucky ones manage to find jobs and earn money to send back to their families. The less fortunate get arrested on arrival and deported, all their efforts in vain. Too many never reach Spain at all but are drowned at sea.

In the 1990s, southern Spain became attractive to two new groups of immigrants. As the EU expanded, Eastern Europeans could legally come to Spain in search of opportunities not available in their own countries. Some brought with them much-needed practical skills.

South Americans, meanwhile, have been flocking to Spain for the last few years because it is a richer, more stable country than their own, and yet still Spanish-speaking.

All the while there has been immigration from the north for an entirely different motivation. People from the wealthy countries of northwest Europe (including Britain, Scandinavia and Germany), who can afford to change their place of residence out of choice rather than the necessity of finding work, are drawn by sunshine and the promise of easy living. Here, they settle on the coasts or buy old village houses inland to do up. Not all of them seek to integrate and instead they often form parallel communities based on countries of origin, each with its own shops, newspapers and radio stations.

All these immigrants bring with them both rewards and problems. The rich ones bring an injection of hard currency but put up property prices. The poor ones supply cheap labour in agriculture and construction when times are good but can become mouths to feed in time of unemployment. Some of them also turn to begging and crime, which is all the harder for the police to deal with because of language and cultural obstacles. And while diversity can be seen as a form of richness, schoolteachers have to cope daily with classes in which not all children share the same mother tongue.

If Andalucians have proved so tolerant of immigration it may be because they see it as inevitable. Geography and history have made their region a transit port between continents and cultures.

The British community is particularly present on the Costa del Sol

Cádiz and Costa de la Luz

Spain's little-visited Atlantic Costa de la Luz – 'coast of light' – is one of the best-kept secrets in Europe. Although the great Río Guadalquivir estuary and a number of ports interrupt it, its 200km (125-mile) beach is the longest – and cleanest – in Spain, and perhaps the whole of southern Europe. Its climate is also kinder than you might expect from an Atlantic coastline.

Stretching from medieval Tarifa (*see pp68–9*) to Isla Cristina near the Portuguese border, the Costa de la Luz is made up of the coasts of two provinces, Cádiz and Huelva. It passes two of Spain's greatest seaports, the largest bird and nature reserve in Europe, Roman ruins, various grand seaside towns and the most unspoilt beaches in the whole of Spain.

History

As the handsome Roman ruins of Bolonia (*see p71*) north of Tarifa's world-class surf beaches (*see pp68–9*) attest, explorers had rounded the Pillars of Hercules to explore Atlantic Spain as early as the 2nd century BC. Bolonia became famous throughout the empire for a spicy fish paste, garum, used as a relish by the wealthier classes.

Even earlier settlers such as the Phoenicians had already brought viniculture to the region, at Cádiz and elsewhere, and fishing ports at Zahara de los Atunes and its neighbour, Barbate. The latter does, however, have one major claim to fame: nearby Cabo de Trafalgar overlooked the 1805 battle which saw the British fleet under Nelson defeat the French and Spanish, although at some personal cost to the admiral.

Coast of Cádiz

The main reason that the Costa de la Luz is one of Europe's best-kept secrets is that holidaymakers from Seville, Cádiz, Huelva and elsewhere tend to keep resorts such as **Conil de la Frontera** and **Chiclana de la Frontera** to themselves. Both are classic bucket-and-spade resorts, although Conil has a photogenic town square and medieval tower with connections to the legend of Guzmán the Good, defender of Tarifa (*see p69*).

The coast of light vanishes beneath the salty lagoons of Cádiz to re-emerge at the garish resort of **Rota**, a favourite for US servicefolk on R&R, and the golden strands of **Chipiona**.

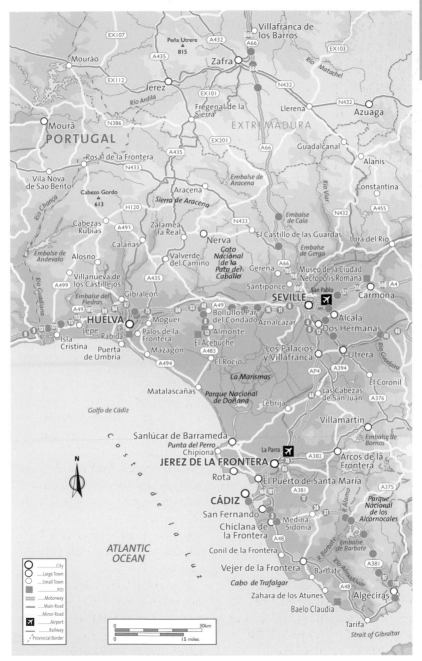

Cádiz and Costa de la Luz

Boats in the bay at Cádiz

However, given the proximity of **Sanlúcar de Barrameda**, you should push on to this atmospheric town with its mansions, *manzanilla bodegas* and fine beaches.

Coast of Huelva

Huelva is the westernmost of the eight Andalucian provinces. Its short coast from **Matalascañas** (at the northern limit of Doñana National Park) to the Portuguese border has some fine deserted beaches backed by sand dunes, punctuated by only two or three resorts – **Mazagón, Puerta de Umbria** and **Isla Cristina**. The city of **Huelva** itself isn't remarkable, but makes a useful base from which to explore the Columbus sites nearby. Inland Huelva, however, has some attractive countryside, particularly in the **Sierra de Aracena**. Huelva's most famous town, **El Rocío**, is well worth a visit at Whitsun, when it is the objective of Andalucía's famous mass pilgrimage (*see p21*).

Cádiz

Said to be the oldest city in Europe, Cádiz has character, history, culture and lifestyle to give Seville a run for its money. Once notorious as a sleazy port, it has tidied up its act over the decades while retaining the tang of its racier times. Isolated on a slender promontory jutting into the Atlantic, it is renowned for its Carnaval that takes place in February or March.

The old town of Cádiz, north of the monumental Puertas de Tierra gates, is a maze of weather-worn mansions and monuments. A narrow street, variously named as it winds around the town, circles the seafront, and connects, for example, the RENFE station on Plaza Sevilla, the Bahía de Cádiz beach, the exquisite Parque del Genovés topiary gardens and the modern *parador*, the Playa de la Caleta and the Plaza de la Catedral. The city centre between these can be traversed in a matter of minutes.

As well as its historic Carnaval, Cádiz has a very lively university culture supporting music venues, clubs, book and music stores, and a high-profile gay community who are the life and soul of Carnaval. It also goes without saying that Cádiz is a fish-eater's paradise: only a fool would leave Cádiz without sampling either the restaurant or tapas bar at its legendary **El Faro** (*Calle San Felix 15*).

Castillo de Santa Catalina

At the north end of the bay, matching the Sebastián sea defences across the bay, sits the citadel of Santa Catalina, built in 1598, which is also a venue for concerts. The fortifications overlook one of Cádiz's most popular beaches, the **Playa de la Caleta** on the left. On the right, the exquisitely sculpted topiary walkways of **Parque del Genovés** look like a backdrop out of a de Chirico painting. The park has a café and an open-air theatre.
Open: daily 10.30am–7.45pm (closes
(*Cont. on p58*)

The Columbus connection

History may have changed its attitude towards 15th-century explorer Christopher Columbus recently, but he remains very much a hero in western Andalucía. He sailed from Palos de la Frontera (near Huelva), Seville, Cádiz and Sanlúcar de Barrameda respectively on his four voyages to the Americas, and is celebrated in statuary and other monuments throughout the region.

Born in Genoa, Italy, in 1451, Cristóbal Colón, as he is known in Spain, gained his reputation as an adventurer in the Mediterranean and Iberian Atlantic before deciding to search for the fabled westerly route to the Orient. Portugal rebuffed his proposal, but the Spanish monarchs Isabel and Fernando (the former especially) agreed to fund his expedition.

Columbus returned from one of his four expeditions to the Americas a criminal in chains, following his disastrous mismanagement of an uprising, and his treatment of indigenous Americans was appalling, if par for the era. Yet his piracy and plunder funded Spain's Golden Age, and sketched out a map of geopolitics still discernible today.

La Rábida

This monastery at the mouth of the Río Tinto estuary south of Huelva is the main Columbus site in Andalucía. He visited the monastery while pursuing support for his expedition, debating with its theologians and seeking divine guidance for his schemes. Today, the monastery is part of a larger theme park-like enclosure, with gardens, exhibits, and replicas of the caravels *Santa María*, *Niña* and *Pinta* with which he sailed on his first voyage in 1492.

Guided tours of the monastery run almost hourly each day, taking in his living quarters, murals of the expeditions and the chapel where fellow explorer Martín Alonso Pinzón, captain of the *Pinta*, is interred.

The replicas of Columbus's three ships are moored at the **Muelle de las Carabelas** (caravel pier), where there is also an exhibit dedicated to his life and exploits.

Monasterio de La Rábida: 8km (5 miles) south of Huelva on N442. Tel: 959 35 04 11. www.monasteriodelarabida.com. Open: Tue–Sun 10am–1pm & 4–6.15pm, closes 7pm in summer

(hourly tours). Closed: Mon. Admission charge.
Replicas of Columbus' ships: Muelle de las Carabelas, open: summer Tue–Fri 10am–2pm & 5–9pm, Sat & Sun 11am–8pm; winter Tue–Sun 9am–7pm. Admission charge.

Palos de la Frontera

This small village is the port from which Columbus and his crew left in 1492. The captains of the *Pinta* and *Niña*, cousins Martín and Vicente Yañez Pinzón, came from here, and they and their crews are commemorated in a monument outside the beautiful town church, where Columbus and his men celebrated Communion on the eve of departure, and in the **Museo Martín Alonso Pinzón** in the town centre.
Museo Martín Alonso Pinzón: Calle Cristóbal Colón 24.

Open: Mon–Fri 10am–2pm. Free admission.

Moguer

This immensely atmospheric, if slightly crumbly, town further inland on the Río Tinto is where many of the three ships' crews came from. The most noteworthy connection with the Columbus legend is the **Monasterio de Santa Clara**, where he honoured a promise, made when he was spared a storm that nearly wrecked the enterprise off the Azores, to keep a vigil for a night on his return from the 1492 voyage.
Monasterio de Santa Clara: Plaza de las Monjas. Tel: 959 37 01 07.
Open: guided visits Tue–Fri at 11am, noon, 1pm, 5pm, 6pm & 7pm by appointment only. Closed: Mon, bank holidays & some Sat for private functions. Admission charge.

Replica boats at La Rábida, near Huelva

8.45pm in summer and 6pm when there are concerts). Free admission.

Catedral Nueva

Cádiz's cathedral, called the 'new' cathedral because it sits on the site of an earlier church, is a mountainous Baroque and neoclassical edifice looming magnificently over the Plaza de la Catedral. Its bright yellow-orange tiled cupola and its towers act as a guidance beacon wherever you walk across town. Although of minor historic detail, it is noted as the last resting place of probably the most famous *gaditano*, as the people of Cádiz are known, composer Manuel de Falla (1876–1946).
Plaza de la Catedral.
Open: Mon–Fri 10am–6.30pm, Sat 10am–4.30pm,
Sun 1–6.30pm. Free admission.

The Catedral Nueva from the seafront

Museo de Cádiz

Near the cathedral, comprising the Museo de Bellas Artes and the Museo Arqueológico, this museum dedicated to the history and culture of Cádiz tracks the city's development from prehistoric times to the present day. On its second floor is a sizeable art gallery, dedicated to works by Murillo, Rubens and Zurbarán.

Plaza de Mina. Tel: 956 20 33 68. Open: Tue 2.30–8.30pm, Wed–Sat 9am–8.30pm, Sun 9.30am–2.30pm. Admission charge, but free to EU citizens.

Oratorio de San Felipe Neri

This Baroque church is one of Cádiz's landmarks. This is the place where the Cortes (parliament) met and created Spain's historic 1812 Constitution. Destroyed by an earthquake in 1755, it was rebuilt in 1764. Above the altar hangs Murillo's **Immaculate Conception**, considered one of the painter's best works.

Calle Santa Inés. Open: Mon–Sat 10am–1pm. Free admission.

Plaza de España

Much of historic Cádiz is centred around the Plaza de España, which is dominated by the **Monumento a las Cortes Liberales,** the monument to Spain's first liberal government, established briefly in Cádiz in the 1810s before being quashed by the monarchy. Beyond it lies the seafront of the Puerto Comercial; northwards,

Plaza de España

steps lead up on to modern-day defences with views over the town.

Puertas de Tierra

These monumental walls were part of the city's 18th-century defences when Andalucía's world trade centre moved to Cádiz from Seville following the silting of the Río Guadalquivir. On the seashore, near the Puertas de Tierra, is the Cárcel Vieja, the old prison.

Torre Tavira

This 18th-century watchtower in the heights above the city is just one of the numerous military installations that offer views back over Cádiz. It features a camera obscura with a 360-degree panorama of the city.

Calle Marqués de Real Tesoro.

(*Cont. on p62*)

Carnaval

Wherever you go in Andalucía in the week running up to Lent, you will find communities large and small celebrating Carnaval, although none of them with the vigour of Cádiz. Carnaval was originally the last chance to unwind before the 40 days of austerity, although few people nowadays observe Lent.

Community and religious groups, professional and youth organisations, and groups of friends roam the streets (usually in the evening and late at night) entertaining crowds, bars and restaurants with pithy and sometimes rude or libellous satirical songs on events of the day. Most groups will enter competitions judged in the town theatres, such as Cádiz's Teatro Falla, while others just take to the streets for the hell of it. Others seize the opportunity to run amok in drag, fancy dress, or as *gigantes*, blobby monsters wielding balloons on sticks on a mission to hunt down every child and tourist and wallop them over the head.

The idea, as perhaps is already apparent, is to have as much good-natured fun as is possible this side of getting arrested. And compared to similar events elsewhere in Europe, Andalucía's Carnavales are remarkably good-natured and convivial affairs. Each climaxes in a *cabalgata*, or cavalcade, where, however modest the display, children of every conceivable age find themselves engulfed in blizzards of confetti and confectionery hurled by retinues of the towns' beauty queens from their gaudily decorated floats.

The notoriety of Cádiz's Carnaval, which stems from both its rumbustious seaport culture and its healthy tradition of resistance to state control, is given further resonance by the fact that it was the only Carnaval that Franco was too scared to ban, fearing that a ban might spark insurrection. It is very much a celebration in the hands of the people, and one where the revellers in what was once the most poverty-stricken region of Spain have over the centuries found at least symbolic ways to wreak revenge on bosses, politicians and the hated *caciques* (foremen) of the despised *latifundistas*.

Even on the storm-prone coast, February can be kind and sunny

Members of a choir at the Cádiz Carnaval dressed as medieval knights

during daytimes, although evenings can be distinctly chilly. Most revellers seem to survive on piping-hot food, alcohol, aerobic motion among the crowds in the streets and generously layered undergarments.

Anyone hoping to join the celebrations in Cádiz, and to a lesser degree in Seville and Granada, should begin making accommodation enquiries the preceding autumn – Cádiz's hotels can fill up months ahead for Carnaval. Alternatives include staying in Puerto de Santa María across the Bahía de Cádiz, with ferry connections to Cádiz's old town during daytimes, or further afield in Jerez or Seville. Late-night and early-morning trains to both are often full of revellers returning home from Cádiz, and both cities will also be celebrating their own Carnavales.

Any of the larger cities will provide a launch pad to smaller, local Carnavales, with tourist offices able to supply key days and venues, and which, while modest, offer a glimpse into *la vida Andaluza*. *www.carnavaldecadiz.com*

Tel: 956 21 29 10. www.torretavira.com.
Open: daily 10am–6pm
(closes 8pm mid-May–mid-Sept).
Admission charge.

Parque Nacional Doñana

The largest nature reserve in Spain and one of the largest in Europe, Doñana stretches from Sanlúcar de Barrameda's shore halfway to Seville, north as far as El Rocío and halfway up to Huelva along the Costa de la Luz. As well as its indigenous wildlife, it is also a stopping-off point for an estimated 6 million migratory birds on their biannual routes north and south in spring and autumn.

Terrain

The Parque Nacional de Doñana was declared a protected area in 1969 for fear that encroaching farming and development might threaten this unique wetland environment. Scientists in fact describe the region as man-made, as over the centuries farming, fishing, hunting and other activities have subtly and not-so-subtly altered its shape and the flora and fauna it supports. The park comprises the *marismas* (marshes) of the Ríos Guadalquivir and Guadiamar, the former here debouching into the Atlantic after its journey from its source 700km (435 miles) away in the Sierra de Cazorla in northwest Andalucía.

Wildlife

As well as its migratory visitors, which in winter months include vast flocks of flamingos feasting on shrimp, the park is also home to fallow and red deer, lynx, boar, mongoose and several rare raptors, including the imperial eagle.

Deer are a common sight at Parque Nacional Doñana

Visiting the park

Visitor numbers in Doñana are strictly limited. If you are just mildly curious or have little time, the best way to get to know a little about the park is to go to one of the five visitors' centres on the edges of the restricted area. The two most accessible are La Rocina and Palacio del Acebrón, both close to the town of El Rocío, but the best one for an introduction to Doñana's wildlife is **El Acebuche** (*open: summer 8am–9pm, closes 7pm in winter*), reached by heading south from El Rocío towards the coast.

The only way to appreciate Doñana fully is to devote time to it and take a guided tour in a 4WD vehicle. This takes 4 hours and ranges over 70km (43 miles), sampling a little of all the ecosystems that make up the park.

An alternative way to visit Doñana is to take a boat trip from the Fábrica de Hielo visitors' centre located at Bajo de Guía (on the outskirts of Sanlúcar de Barrameda). Of course, the wildlife you do or do not see depends on the time of year and luck. Mammals are particularly difficult to see but birds are more visible, especially during the spring and autumn migrations.
Guided 4WD tours. Trips leave from El Acebuche visitors' centre.
Tel: 959 43 04 32.
Tours depart: Jul–mid-Sept Mon–Sat 8.30am & 5pm; mid-Sept–Jun Tue–Sun 8.30am & 3pm. Booking essential.
Boat trips. Tel: 956 36 38 13.
www.visitasdonana.com.

Departures from Bajo de Guía: Nov–Mar 10am; Apr–May & Oct 10am & 4pm; Jun–Sept 10am & 5pm. Visits take 3½ hours. Reservations essential.

Jerez de la Frontera

Jerez is the quintessential Andalucian town, the home to *fino* (dry) sherry and to a *gitano* flamenco culture second only to that of Seville, and the birthplace of classical, horseback bullfighting, still practised today in its bullring. It is also very British, thanks to the presence of sherry dynasties such as Harvey, Williams & Humbert, Domecq, González Byass, Sandeman and others.

There has been a human settlement on the site of Jerez since Phoenician times. The Romans named it Xeres, the Moors Scheris, from which both *jerez* (Spanish for sherry) and sherry derive. The dry white fortified wines produced from the grapes of its temperate vineyards made it the leader of the three key sherry-producing towns in Andalucía (*see pp66–7*). The sherry trade also made its sherry dynasties extremely wealthy, a wealth reflected in the monuments and great houses of the town's centre.

Being so close to the great port of Cádiz, it is perhaps unsurprising that Jerez is rather industrial. The centre, however, offers the visitor a few architectural delights.

Centro Andaluz de Flamenco

Jerez sits near the delta of the Río Guadalquivir valley, which gave

Seville and Cádiz their distinctive flamenco cultures. The city's Centro Andaluz de Flamenco is a library, archive, museum and school of flamenco dedicated to keeping the tradition alive beyond the commercialised *tablaos* of the big cities. On most summer season mornings, the centre shows an hourly audiovisual presentation on the history of flamenco.
Plaza de San Juan.
Tel: 856 81 41 32.
www.centroandaluzdeflamenco.es.
Open: Mon–Fri 9am–2pm.
Free admission.

The Old Quarter

Numerous monuments jostle for attention in the historic centre. The **Alcázar**, or fortress, is smaller than those in Almería, Málaga and elsewhere but is well preserved and boasts a camera obscura offering half-hourly panoramic views over the city. (*Alameda Vieja. Open: Nov–Jan daily 10am–3pm; Feb–mid-Jul & mid-Sept–Oct Mon–Sat 10am–6pm, Sun 10am–3pm; mid-Jul–mid-Sept Mon–Fri 10am–8pm, Sat & Sun 10am–3pm. Admission charge*).

Visible downhill from the Alcázar is the town's **Catedral**, whose Gothic basilica was completed in the 18th century. However, the cathedral dates back to the Mudéjar period, notably the free-standing bell tower (*Plaza de la Encarnación. Open: daily 11am–1pm. Free admission*).

Real Escuela Andaluza de Arte Ecuestre

Jerez's annual May Feria del Caballo (horse fair) is the biggest country fair in the entire Andalucian calendar. Outside the *feria*, the city's famous Real Escuela Andaluza de Arte Ecuestre is Andalucía's premier school for training horses and riders. Some mornings you can observe dressage practice, and on Thursday mornings the school also stages a performance in which horses and riders are accompanied by classical music.

The Gothic cathedral has parts dating back to before the Reconquest

The Alcázar in the Old Quarter

Avenida Duque de Abrantes.
Tel: 956 31 96 35. www.realescuela.org.
Open: Mon, Wed & Fri 10am–2pm
Sept–Jul. Full performances normally
Tue, Thur & Fri noon, but check in
advance. Admission charge.

Sherry *bodegas*

The Alcázar overlooks two of Jerez's most famous *bodegas*, Domecq and González Byass. They and the Harveys, Sandeman, Wisdom & Warter and Williams & Humbert *bodegas* (all within walking distance) offer tours and tastings (mostly mornings). Booking is advisable.
Alvaro Domecq: Calle San Luís.
Tel: 956 33 96 34.
www.alvarodomecq.com. Guided tours by
appointment only Mon–Fri 11am,
12.30pm & 2pm. Admission charge.
González Byass: Calle Manuel González.
Tel: 902 44 00 77.

www.gonzalezbyass.com. Tours in English
Mon–Sat noon, 1pm, 2pm, 5pm &
6.30pm; Sun noon, 1pm, 2pm
(more tours in summer).
Admission charge.
Harveys: Pintor Muñoz Cebrión.
Tel: 956 31 29 95.
www.bodegasharveys.com.
Tours Mon–Fri noon.
Admission charge.
Sandeman: Calle Pizarro.
Tel: 956 15 17 00. www.sandeman.com.
Tours in English Mon, Wed & Fri hourly
11.30am–2.30pm; Tue & Thur 10.30am,
noon, 1pm, 2pm & 3pm.
Sat by appointment.
Admission charge.
Williams & Humbert: Calle Nuño de
Cañas. Tel: 956 35 34 06.
www.williams-humbert.com.
Open: Mon–Fri 10am, noon &
1.30pm; evenings, Sat & Sun by
appointment only. Admission charge.

The Sherry Triangle

Wine and, in particular, sherry has been produced in western Andalucía for at least 3,000 years, having been introduced by Phoenician traders. Under Greek and Roman invaders, the Jerez region became a centre for sherry production and export throughout the Mediterranean. The teetotal Moors were largely indifferent to its alcoholic qualities, although their medicinal alembic, or still, would later find non-medical uses in distilleries around the globe.

British wine traders arrived in the pacified Spain following the Reconquest and set about carving up the sherry trade. The region's dry, chalky soil, temperate mix of sunshine and Atlantic weather systems, and, most importantly of all, the *solera* (vintage, or traditional) production process made it perfect for producing sweet (*oloroso*) and dry (*fino*) sherries. Three towns or areas make up the so-called Sherry Triangle: Sanlúcar de Barrameda, Jerez and the area around Cádiz and El Puerto de Santa María.

There are five main types of sherry, including the *oloroso* and *fino*. The latter, typified by brands such as Domecq's La Ina, is by far the more popular in bars and as an aperitif,

usually drunk chilled from the fridge. *Amontillado* is a stronger form of *fino*, one in which the *flor* (yeast) has been allowed to develop a richer, sometimes dry, sometimes sweet, taste. Cream, most famously bottled as Harvey's Bristol Cream, is a blend of *oloroso* and sun-dried Ximénez grapes.

Sherry production follows that of wine, with two crucial later stages. During fortification, distilled grape spirit is added, which increases alcohol content to 18 per cent for sweet and 15 per cent for dry. The sherry is stored for three months in wooden barrels where young sherry is gradually filtered down through a succession of barrels containing older sherry. The final mix of old and young is then bottled. Other random processes – the quality of harvest, the appearance of flor, and the drying of grapes for Pedro Ximénez dessert sherry – also produce variations on the *oloroso/fino* process.

Manzanilla, produced exclusively in the handsome seaside town of Sanlúcar de Barrameda on the mouth of the Guadalquivir, is considered an entirely different type of sherry. Aficionados insist that its light, drier

Sherry is stored for three months in wooden barrels

taste is far superior to *fino*. *Manzanilla* is unfortified, and romantic myth claims that its special flavour comes from salty sea breezes blowing in across the vineyards. A more likely explanation would be soil, irrigation and climate. Just as in Jerez, Sanlúcar's *manzanilla bodegas*, such as La Guita, offer guided tours and tastings.

The third point of the Sherry Triangle is the area around Cádiz and neighbouring El Puerto de Santa María (a fast-developing tourist alternative to Cádiz itself, and served by a swift ferry service), which both produce *fino* from vineyards in the surrounding Guadalquivir valley.

Fino and *manzanilla* are the Andalucian tipple of choice for socialising. One of the best ways to sample *manzanilla* is at the huge tapas festival that takes place on Sanlúcar's central boulevard, Alzado de Ejército, in the second week of October. The Andalucian passion for *jerez* reaches its peak during the fiestas such as the *ferias* that take place in the different cities over the summer, which are staggered at different dates: townsfolk hang *copitas* (small glasses in leather holsters) around their necks and share bottles among themselves as they carouse in the streets.

Kite-surfing, mixing parachuting with windsurfing, at Tarifa beach

Tarifa and the Surf Coast

It may be stuck on an extreme tip of southern Europe but the medieval town of Tarifa has managed to draw attention to itself. An accident of local winds and tides, an embarrassment of glorious sandy beaches and the efforts of the surfie grapevine have elected it one of the three great surf destinations in the world.

The town is named after its 8th-century invader, Tarif ben Maluk, who made a successful sortie to the European mainland to scout the land for Tariq ibn Ziyad's invasion of Gibraltar in AD 711. While its medieval walls and street plan remain, it has changed rather drastically over the past decade. Every other shopfront in its maze-like walled Moorish old town is a boutique, gear store, cybercafé or bar dedicated to the shrimpcatcher-shorts set. Traditionally a laid-back hideaway, popular with backpackers on their way to and from North Africa, its New Age emporia now find themselves serving a new generation of beach bums.

Tarifa is also, unsurprisingly, a party town, nowhere more so than in the bars, cafés and restaurants around Calle Sancho IV in the centre. It is also worth pointing out that while some of its best hotels, such as La Casa Amarilla and La Sacristia, are here, most visitors head for the beach hotels such as the Hurricane and Dos Mares a dozen or so kilometres north.

Tarifa's beaches themselves begin unprepossessingly but improve around the Hurricane hotel and are at their best by the dune systems of Valdevaqueros, where hardcore surfers can be found at play year-round.

Castillo de Guzmán

Parts of the handsome ramparts are still used by the Spanish naval authorities and off-limits to visitors, but Tarifa's most imposing structure, the Castillo de Guzmán, has undergone heavy restoration and has been reopened to the public. Built on the site of a 10th-century Moorish Alcázar, itself built on the site of a Roman fort, this was rebuilt as a *Reconquista* castle in the 11th century. The castle acquired its name and its place in history during the 1292 Moorish siege of Tarifa, when the Christians defended the town against invaders from Morocco. Its name derives from the honorific title awarded by the people to Alonso Pérez Guzmán, Guzmán el Bueno (Guzmán the Good), the castle's commander, who sacrificed his son, who had been taken hostage by the invaders, rather than surrender the town.
Guzmán el Bueno. Tel: 956 68 09 93.

Open: Tue–Sat 11am–2pm & 5–7pm, Sun 11am–2pm. Admission charge.

Iglesia de San Francisco

This 16th-century church on the Plaza del Angel, on the west side of the old town, was restored at the end of the 18th century. It contains the Cristo del Desconsuelo, a 15th-century sculpture of Christ.
Plaza del Angel. Open: Wed–Fri 7.30am–8.30pm, Sun 7am–1pm. Free admission.

Iglesia de San Mateo

Also of interest is the Iglesia de San Mateo, on the corner of calles Moscardo and Copons, begun in the 15th century but only completed in the 18th. The dilapidated Baroque exterior conceals a surprisingly modern interior.
Open: daily 8.30am–1pm & 5.30–9pm. Free admission.

Whale watching

As well as surfie boutiques, Tarifa has more than its fair share of emporia offering dolphin- and whale-watching expeditions. The most ecologically sound thing to do would be to leave these beautiful creatures in peace, but if you have to see them it's best to go with non-profit-making organisations such as **Whale Watch** (*Avenida de la Constitución 6. Tel: 956 62 70 13. www.whalewatchtarifa.net*) or **Aventura Marina** (*Avenida Andalucía 1. Tel: 956 68 19 32. www.aventuramarina.org*).

Roman Andalucía

Andalucía occupied a position of great privilege in the western Roman Empire for 500 years from the 2nd century BC to the 3rd century AD. Following centuries of rule by Carthage, the great Mediterranean force in what is nowadays Tunisia, the inhabitants of the southwestern tip of the peninsula welcomed the Roman invaders, and certainly thrived on the culture they introduced. Roman Baetica, as the region was known, was almost identical in outline to modern-day Andalucía.

The windswept Roman ruins of Ronda la Vieja, 'Old Ronda'

Carthage was already on the wane when the Romans invaded this part of the peninsula in the last decade of the 3rd century BC. They began construction of their greatest settlement, Italica, just north of Seville, in 206 BC. The thriving seaport at modern-day Bolonia, Baelo Claudia (named after the emperor Claudius), followed. So, in the 1st century AD, did Acinipo, the extensive ruined settlement on a windswept bluff outside Ronda, as **Ronda la Vieja** (Old Ronda).

Italica

At its height, around the 1st century AD, Italica was one of the greatest cities in the Roman Empire, a rival to even Alexandria and Rome. Its population reached half a million, and its monumental amphitheatre, visible in part today, held in excess of 25,000 people. The Visigoths simply abandoned the site for their preferred base of Seville, while later rulers plundered the site for materials (including the stone columns that now surround Seville Cathedral). Also still visible are the vestiges of several halls and mosaics, foundations and men's and women's baths.

Santiponce. 5km (3 miles) north of Seville. Open: Apr–Sept Tue–Sat 8.30am–9pm, Sun 9am–3pm; Oct–Mar Tue–Sat 9am–6.30pm, Sun 10am–4pm. Admission charge, but free to EU citizens.

Baelo Claudia

This smaller but less vandalised site sits on the beach at Bolonia north of Tarifa. Although less impressive than Italica, it includes the remains of a forum, baths, an open-air auditorium, temples to Juno, Jupiter and Minerva, and other religious buildings. Near the beach is the vestigial fish factory responsible for garum, an alarming paste of fish parts that was shipped throughout the Roman Empire and revered as the best caviar is today.

Baelo Claudia, Bolonia beach. 15km (9 miles) north of Tarifa on N340. Open: Mar–May & Oct Tue–Sat 10am–7pm; Jun–Sept Tue–Sat 10am–9pm; Nov–Feb Tue–Sat 10am–6pm; Sun 9am–2pm all year. Admission charge.

Acinipo/Ronda la Vieja

Known by either of these names on local maps and road signs, this has one of the most spectacular settings in the whole of Andalucía: it lies on a slope rising to one of a series of bluffs above rolling farmland east of Ronda, with views of the sierras to the north.

A dig in progress like Baelo Claudia, Acinipo has so far yielded a magnificent open-air theatre and auditorium, the groundworks of a triple hot-water baths, fragments of a forum, a skeletal street grid and piles of what were once the rock walls of the town itself. Its remote site left it prone to ransackers over the centuries.

Acinipo, on MA-499 Ronda–Setenil. Tel: 670 945 451. Open: Tue–Sun 9am–5pm, but times may vary so check by phone. Free admission.

Backstage at the monumental theatre in Roman Acinipo

Pueblos Blancos and Valle de Grazalema

Visiting the Pueblos Blancos from Seville, Ronda or the Costa del Sol depends on two things: time and transport. With a car the main pueblos could be seen in a couple of days, although the driver would be missing some of the finest landscapes in Andalucía. With time, using public transport and the odd taxi is an ideal way to tour the villages. It's even possible to tour them by cycle or on foot.

Arcos de la Frontera

Arcos is the most impressive of the Pueblos Blancos after Ronda. It too sits on its own defensive bluff, 100m (328ft) above the Río Guadalete and is something of a geological anomaly in the surroundings of gentle rolling farmland.

Arcos's compact *casco antiguo* (old town) is barely a five-minute walk across in any direction, but its narrow streets and alleys bulge with marvels over a thousand years old. The **Castillo de los Duques**, named after the family that owned Arcos for centuries, dates back to the 11th century, although its interior is closed to the public. The 15th-century **Iglesia de San Pedro** bell tower has a deafening triple carillon that stops people in their tracks on the hour. The **Convento de la Encarnación** and the **Palacio del Conde de Águila** are among the oldest façades.

From Arcos there are two roads east to Ronda. The main road skirts the Embalse de Bornos reservoir, but a more scenic route is over the hills via El Bosque, Benamahoma and Grazalema.

Iglesia de San Pedro: Calle Núñez de Prado. Open: Mon–Fri 10.30am–2pm & 5–7pm, Sat 10.30am–2pm. Closed: Sun. Admission charge.

Casares

Below Gaucín, on another peak between the village and the coast, is tiny Casares. Another classic tangle of whitewashed alleys on a mountain, it is notable chiefly as the birthplace of Blas Infante, the founder of the Andalucismo regional autonomy movement in the 1930s.

Cueva de la Pileta

The Cueva de la Pileta, near the town of Benaoján, can only be visited on an hour-long guided tour. Inside it are some superb prehistoric paintings and what appears to be an ancient form of writing, the origins and purposes of which have yet to be explained. Another cave, **El Gato**, on the other side of Benaoján, has a dramatic entrance which is open to all but its depths are the preserve of the experienced cave diver.

Cueva de la Pileta. 4.5km (3 miles) from Benaoján towards Cortes de la Frontera. Tel: 952 16 73 43. Departures from entrance when sufficient numbers of people have gathered to form a group, daily 10am–1pm & 4–6pm, closes 5pm in winter. Admission charge.

Gaucín

Southwest of Ronda, the A369 leads to another pretty town, Gaucín, which is also an ideal base from which to explore the area. These barren mountainscapes proved ideal hiding places for fugitive Moors during the Reconquest, and many of the villages here bear the prefix 'Ben' – Benadalid, Benalauria, Benarraba – from the Arabic *ibn* (son of). Gaucín is now a sizeable artists' colony.

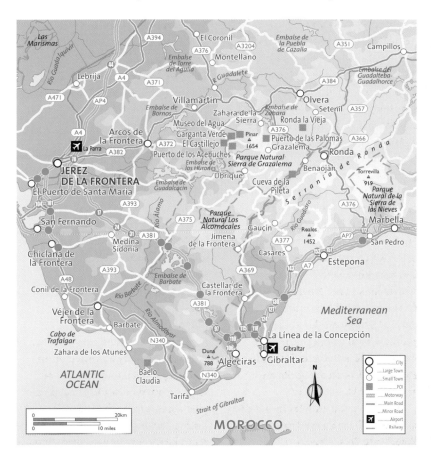

The El Gato cave system outside Benaoján

Grazalema

Grazalema has the dubious honour of receiving the highest amount of rainfall in Spain, but at least that keeps the countryside green. The town is attractive in itself and serves as a base for hiking in the nature reserve named after it (*see pp75 & 78–9*), which is good for birdwatching and botanising.

Artesanía Textil de Grazalema keeps up the local weaving industry, making blankets and ponchos on hand looms in its small factory, which can be visited (*Carretera de Ronda. Tel: 956 13 20 08. www.mantasdegrazalema.es. Open: Sept–Jun Mon–Thur 8am–2pm & 3–6.30pm, Fri 8am–2pm; Jul daily 7am–3pm. Closed: Aug*).

Jimena de la Frontera

West beyond Gaucín, before the sierras flatten out towards Gibraltar, is the pleasant hill town of Jimena de la Frontera, with another fortress from the centuries of the Reconquest.

To the north and southwest of Gaucín and Jimena is the remote expanse of the Parque Natural Los Alcornocales, a nature reserve that includes the biggest extension of cork trees in Spain – their bark being harvested to make bottle corks. There are visitor centres for the reserve at **Alcalá de los Gazules** (*Calle Los Pozos. Tel: 956 42 03 30*) and **Cortes de la Frontera** (*Avenida de la Democracia. Tel: 952 15 45 99*).

Medina Sidonia

Medina Sidonia, another hilltop redoubt, is famed as the seat awarded to the family of Guzmán el Bueno (Guzmán the Good), defender of Tarifa (*see p69*). The palace of the Duques de Medina Sidonia is now the home of a Foundation to protect its cultural heritage. It also has a cafeteria and guest rooms available (*www.fcmedinasidonia.com*).

The town's central Plaza de España is home to both an impressive 17th-century *ayuntamiento* (town council) building and Medina Sidonia's star attraction, the **Iglesia de Santa María la Coronada**, which contains some remarkable votary art and details dating back to the period in the 16th century when it also served as local headquarters for the Inquisition. The ruins of Roman sewers, still visible on the outskirts of town, suggest that Medina Sidonia was an important settlement in pre-Christian times, and its three monumental Moorish gates suggest that it also held a similar office prior to the Reconquest.

Palacio de Medina Sidonia, Plaza Condesa de Niebla 1. Tel: 956 36 01 61. Open: for guided visits only Sun 11am & noon. Admission charge.

Olvera

North of Setenil, Olvera is interesting for its church, and its reputation as one of the worst 19th-century bandit lairs.

Parque Natural Sierra de Grazalema

The limestone bedrock of the area of mountains now protected as the Parque Natural Sierra de Grazalema, and its position equidistant between the Atlantic and Mediterranean, has given rise to a unique and vulnerable

(*Cont. on p78*)

Pueblos Blancos and Valle de Grazalema

The picturesque village of Olvera sits on top of a hill

Los bandoleros (bandits)

As recently as the 1950s the mountains of the Serranía de Ronda were still known as bandit country, although these bandits were a somewhat different breed from the highwaymen of the 18th and 19th centuries. The treacherous mountain routes between Algeciras and Gibraltar and the cities of Seville, Málaga and Granada had long been favoured by *contrabandistas* (smugglers), bringing illicit supplies ashore and spiriting them through the high mountain passes. In the 1940s and 50s, the bandits shared the mountain paths with fugitive 'Reds', soldiers of the defeated Republican brigades fleeing the vengeance of Franco's henchmen after the Civil War (*see pp90–91*) and eking out an existence at these inhospitable altitudes.

Banditry probably first appeared in Andalucía around the 12th century, where we might date the decisive swing in favour of the Christians during the long centuries of the Reconquest. These first bandits were fugitive Moors fleeing persecution, or at least forced conversion. By the 18th century, with the majority of Moors either assimilated or expelled, the bandits tended to be disenfranchised or disgruntled peasants or disgraced gentry forced to flee into the hills after committing murders or other hanging offences. The Pueblos Blancos were notorious bandit lairs, including Gaucín and, most notorious of all, Olvera, which actually features in a

The barren Serranía de Ronda

famous saying of the period: 'Kill your man and flee to Olvera.'

Perhaps inevitably, many of these figures acquired a romantic, Robin Hood-like, status, and their system of exacting money from the unwary rich if they ventured unwisely into the mountains would certainly have struck a welcome chord with the region's poor. One such, José Alloa Tragabuches, was a famous Ronda bullfighter and a pupil of Pedro Romero (see p82). Myths about Tragabuches vary: in one he killed a rival matador and fled justice, while in another he killed an unfaithful wife or girlfriend in a fit of jealous rage and headed for Olvera.

Another bandit, José María Hinojosa Cabacho, nicknamed El Tempranillo, was a media legend in his own time, and was even given to issuing his own press releases, once declaring that while the king might rule Spain, El Tempranillo ruled the sierras. When wealthy northern Europeans began to tour Andalucía in the 19th century, figures such as El Tempranillo were even contacted by rich tourists willing to pay for the thrill of being 'held up' by a bona fide bandit. And when El Tempranillo married a young woman from (and in) Grazalema, the authorities are said to have turned a blind eye while the nuptials took place.

Entrance to the Bandit Museum in Ronda

The romantic form of banditry began to die out in the mid-19th century, due largely to drastic measures taken by the state. However, for a long time after the Civil War had ended and even when democracy had returned to Spain, rumours kept circulating about ageing, renegade 'Red' soldiers hiding out in the sierras, living off the land and avoiding the Guardia Civil, unaware that hostilities were over. Fact or myth, it all makes for some good stories. The lives and reputations, histories and legends, of all the rogues, rovers, fugitives and folk heroes who lived and died in the sierras are celebrated in a museum in Ronda, the **Museo del Bandolero** (*Calle Armiñan. Tel: 952 87 77 85. www.museobandolero.com. Open: daily 10.30am–8pm, closes 7pm in winter. Admission charge*).

combination of geology, flora and fauna. The park covers 52,000 hectares (130,000 acres), roughly bounded by the towns of El Bosque, Algodonales, Ronda and Cortes de la Frontera, and merges to the southwest with the Parque Natural Los Alcornocales (*see p74*).

Star of the park's flora and fauna is *Abies pinsapo*, the Spanish fir tree (*pinsapo* in Spanish), which only grows above 1,000m (3,280ft) and is a relic of the forests of the Tertiary era. Far more spectacular are the eagles which fly over the mountains, but the most conspicuous bird you are likely to see, still impressive as it soars on thermal currents of air, is the griffon vulture.

Where to go

You can get a glimpse of the scenery and perhaps the wildlife through a car window, especially if you stop at one of the viewpoints which are located at Cintillo (Benaocaz, near Ubrique), **Puerto de las Palomas** and **Puerto de los Acebuches** (both near Grazalema); but you will perhaps enjoy your visit more if you follow one of the 15 marked walking routes. The most popular is to **Garganta Verde**, a gorge popular with canyoners and home to a colony of vultures. The footpath following the old road between Grazalema and Benamahoma, over the Puerto de las Cumbres, takes you past some fine woods of Spanish fir.

The wilder parts of Grazalema's park are tightly controlled by the park authorities

Other good places to visit in the park are the botanic garden at **El Castillejo** (El Bosque) and the **Museo del Agua** (Water Museum) in an old watermill at Benamahoma.

Rules and precautions

The Parque Natural Sierra de Grazalema is one of the most accessible of Andalucía's nature reserves, but it is very sensitive to visitor interference and as such is patrolled by wardens. Always keep to marked paths, do not remove plants or even rocks, and leave any animals you come across alone, particularly during the breeding season. And never light a fire: even though these hills receive a high level of rainfall, forest fire is still an ever-present risk.

Ronda

Few towns have a setting as dramatic as Ronda, the most famous of the so-called 'white towns' (Pueblos Blancos) of Andalucía. Not only does it nudge up to a vertiginous cliff, but it also straddles a deep gorge. For its setting alone, Ronda is a magnet for coach parties coming up from the Costa del Sol. Fortunately, it hasn't quite turned into a cliché, although it could easily do so as it promotes itself these days as the cradle of modern bullfighting and the former haunt of *bandoleros*.

Ronda has good road and rail links with Seville and Málaga, and a large choice of hotels and restaurants. As such, it makes an excellent base for

INFORMATION AND GUIDED TOURS

There are three visitor centres for Grazalema's park (in addition to Grazalema tourist information office):

Cortes de la Frontera: *Avenida de la Democracia. Tel: 952 15 45 99.*

El Bosque (useful if coming from the direction of Arcos de la Frontera): *Avenida de la Diputación. Tel: 956 72 70 29.*

Zahara de la Sierra: *Plaza de Zahara 3. Tel: 956 12 31 14.*

Horizon: *Calle Corrales Terceros 29. Tel: 956 13 23 63. www.horizonaventura.com* A private company based in Grazalema that organises walks, excursions and other sports and activities ranging from easy to difficult.

exploring the other white towns that dot the surrounding sierras.

La Ciudad (Old Town)

An anticlockwise route around the old town will lead to the **Palacio de Mondragón**, a renovated Moorish palace now used as town museum, a language school and conference centre with beautiful miniature water gardens (*open: Mon–Fri 10am–7pm, Sat & Sun 10am–3pm. Admission charge*).

Beyond the Mondragón is the handsome **Plaza de Duques de Parcent**, with the unusual arcaded *ayuntamiento* and neighbouring **Santa María la Mayor** church with its Baroque bell tower (*open: Mon–Sat 10am–8pm, Sun 10am–1pm Admission charge*).

Downhill from the Plaza, Armiñán leads to the **Iglesia**

Ronda is perched on top of a cliff

concerts and opera. It is used in early September for the annual Goyesca *corrida*, or bullfight, that is the climax of the September *feria* or fair. Tickets for the Goyesca, in which the participants dress in the manner of Goya's paintings of the bullfight, often sell out in advance, and can be expensive, especially to sit in the *sombra* (shade).
Calle Virgen de la Paz 15. www.rmcr.org. Open: Nov–Feb 10am–6pm; Apr–Sept 10am–8pm; Mar & Oct 10am–7pm. Admission charge.

Espíritu Santo (*open: Mon–Sat 10am–2pm. Admission charge*). Calle Marqués de Salvatierra, off Calle Armiñán, leads down to the **Baños Árabes**, the best-preserved Arab baths in Spain (*Open: Mon–Fri 10am–7pm, Sat & Sun 10am–3pm*).

Plaza de Toros

Famously, Ronda is the birthplace of 'modern', that is, on foot, bullfighting, pioneered by legendary matador Pedro Romero in the town's Plaza de Toros in the 18th century. Today, the Plaza is ~gely a museum and a venue for

Puente Nuevo

Almost every view of Ronda shows the 98m (321ft) -high 'new bridge' striding across the Tajo gorge. It was built in 1793 and is called the 'new' bridge because an earlier attempt to span the gap ended fruitlessly with the deaths of 50 people. The bridge has a visitors' centre inside it. (*Open: Mon–Fri 10am–7pm, Sat & Sun 10am–3pm. Admission charge.*)

Véjer de la Frontera

It has at least two other rivals for the title, but Véjer has to be one of the most exquisite and archetypal of the Pueblos Blancos: a tangle of whitewashed streets and alleys atop a defensive bluff with panoramic views and many of its defences still intact. Although it has an impressive 16th-century church, the **Iglesia del Divino Salvador**, and a castle (*castillo*), the best way to see Véjer is simply to wander its alleys, ramparts and squares, many of them with fantastic views down over the Costa de la Luz. The **Plaza de España** has an outrageous Triana-tiled fountain.

Iglesia del Divino Salvador: Calle Ramón y Cajal (entrance by the back door). Open: daily 11am–1pm & 5–7pm. Closed: Tue & Thur pm. Free admission. Castillo open: daily 11am–7pm. Free admission.

Near Véjer there is an interesting art gallery, the **Fundación NMAC**, where the aim is to show contemporary works of art set against nature.

Fundación NMAC: Dehesa de Montenmedio (off the A48). Tel: 956 45 51 34.

www.fundacionnmac.com. Open: summer Mon–Sat 10am–2pm & 5–8.30pm, Sun 10am–2pm; winter 10am–2.30pm & 4–6pm, Sun 10am–2pm. Admission charge.

Zahara de la Sierra

A car is necessary to reach the breathtaking Puerto de las Palomas (Pass of the Doves) above Grazalema. From here you can look down on little-visited Zahara de la Sierra, on its windswept peak overlooking a vast *embalse*, or reservoir. The obligatory ruined Moorish castle at the top of Zahara's craggy pinnacle is the best preserved in the region.

Véjer de la Frontera's magnificent Plaza de España fountain

Death in the afternoon

Bullfighting probably originated as a gladiatorial sport, pitting man, mounted or on foot, against a single bull, in Roman or Moorish times. It acquired its layers of robing and ritual – the *traje de luces* (suit of lights) that every matador wears, the *picadores* and *banderilleros* who assist the matador – over the

centuries. It was codified in places such as the great equestrian centre Jerez and, later, Ronda in the 18th century, where legendary matador Pedro Romero 'invented' modern, on foot, bullfighting.

The *corrida*

The *corrida* has its rhythms, which are measured out by the *presidente*, the president of the fight or bullring, and accompanying brass band: it is up to the *presidente* to judge the progress of the *corrida*, and to usher the action on through its three key stages. In the case of a particularly disastrous performance by either matador or bull, he can also dismiss either or both from the ring, to the shame of the former, and the crowd can actually petition for a brave bull to be freed, usually by waving white handkerchiefs.

The first stage of the *corrida*, the *tercio de varas*, is the initial engagement between matador and bull, where the former may leave the bull to the goading of his *peones*, unmounted assistants who taunt the bull with capes. They are joined by *picadores*, mounted on padded horses, who engage the bull by

Plaza de Toros, Seville

plunging long lances into its spine, weakening its back and neck muscles.

It is quite common for their heavily padded and blindfolded horses to be flipped by the enraged bull.

In the *tercio de banderillas*, unmounted assistants, *banderilleros*, often in *trajes de luces* themselves, feint at the bull and plunge *bandilleras* (long beribboned darts) into its back, further weakening the animal.

The final stage – if all goes to plan – is the *estocada*, or death blow, where the matador will judge the bull's strength by various passes of the *muleta*, the famed red cape. The perfect *estocada*, rarely seen, is the *estocada recibiendo*, in which the matador allows the bull to charge, meets it and deals a death blow to the spinal column with his sword. Sometimes, however, especially with younger matadors fighting *novilladas*, the *estocada* is not struck, and it is not uncommon for *peones* to have to finish the bull off with a bolt-gun to the forehead before it is dragged from the *plaza de toros*.

A poster advertising bullfights

The future of bullfighting

In modern Spain, bullfighting is regarded as something between a sport and an art form. It is reported in the newspapers, highlights are shown on television and matadors are honoured as celebrities on a par with pop and film stars. While only a minority of Spaniards regularly attend bullfights, a majority of the population seems content to tolerate bullfighting unquestioningly as an inviolable part of Spanish culture, whatever the rest of the world thinks. There are, however, animal rights campaigners who would like to ban bullfighting as cruel and anachronistic, but so far they have not made much progress in winning over public opinion (although the city of Barcelona has declared itself a bullfighting-free zone).

Western Costa del Sol

The Costa del Sol stretches from La Línea de la Concepción, on the border with Gibraltar, to Nerja, Málaga dividing the more developed and more trendy western stretch from its less pretentious eastern counterpart. Parts are blighted by unregulated sprawl, but the 21st-century first-time visitor may be surprised at how much of it remains free of intense high-rise development. And it is noticeable in some places that the Costa del Sol is attracting and providing facilities for a new, discerning, more eco-minded class of tourist.

Málaga

Andalucía's second-largest city after Seville, with a population of over half a million, Málaga is the main airport of entry for visitors, the administrative centre for most government agencies, and the place where you will find overseas consulates or their representatives. Many people fly into and out of Málaga for a holiday on the Costa del Sol without bothering to visit the city itself, but it merits at least a half day's exploration.

Málaga's history stretches back to the Phoenicians, who established it as a key Mediterranean port, a role it has kept through Moorish and Christian rule until the present day. The Phoenicians also introduced viticulture, which blossomed with the city's sweet and fortified wines, but the industry was devastated by the 19th-century phylloxera epidemic. (The Larios family did better with their Málaga-distilled gin, which still beats famous British brands in blindfold tests.)

The city gave Spain and indeed the 20th century its most famous painter, Picasso, and it was the second most fought-over Republican bulwark after Barcelona during the Civil War.

The city centre, bordered by the riverbed, Alameda Principal and calles Carretería and Alamos, is a busy clutch of streets and alleys. Málaga also claims to be a city of gardens, its main one being the Paseo del Parque.

Alcazaba

The city centre is overlooked by this fortress-palace that is entered through a series of horseshoe-shaped gateways. Next to it is an excavated Roman theatre. There are fairly good views over the city from the Alcazaba walls, but much better ones from the castle that stands above it on the crest of the hill, **Gibralfaro**.

Alcazaba: Calle Alcazabilla. Open: summer Tue–Sun 9.30am–8pm; winter Tue–Sun 8.30am–7pm. Admission charge (free Sun after 2pm).

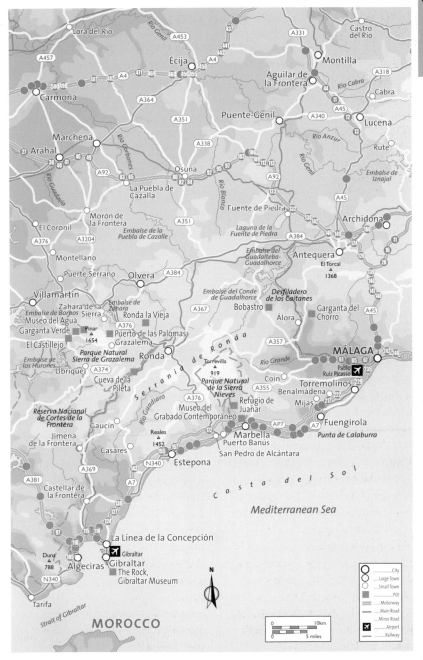

Lora del Río
Castro del Río
Écija
Montilla
Aguilar de la Frontera
Cabra
Carmona
Lucena
Marchena
Rute
Arahal
Osuna
Embalse de Iznajal
La Puebla de Cazalla
Morón de la Frontera
Fuente de Piedra
El Coronil
Archidona
Montellano
Laguna de la Fuente de Piedra
Antequera
Puerto Serrano
Olvera
El Torcal ▲ 1368
Villamartín
Embalse del Guadalteba-Guadalhorce
Embalse del Conde de Guadalhorce
Desfiladero de los Caitanes
Zahara de la Sierra
Garganta del Chorro
Embalse de Bornos
Embalse de Zahara
Ronda la Vieja
Bobastro
Museo del Agua
Álora
Garganta Verde
Pinar ▲ 1654
Puerto de las Palomas
El Castillejo
Grazalema
MÁLAGA
Embalse de los Hurones
Parque Natural Sierra de Grazalema
Ronda
Pablo Ruiz Picasso
Ubrique
Río Grande
Cueva de la Pileta
Torrevilla ▲ 919
Coín
Torremolinos
Reserva Nacional de Cortes de la Frontera
Parque Natural de la Sierra Nieves
Benalmádena
Mijas
Gaucín
Museo del Grabado Contemporáneo
Refugio de Juanar
Fuengirola
Jimena de la Frontera
Reales ▲ 1452
Marbella
Punta de Calaburra
Casares
Puerto Banús
San Pedro de Alcántara
Estepona
Castellar de la Frontera
Costa del Sol
Mediterranean Sea
La Línea de la Concepción
Duna ▲ 788
Gibraltar
Algeciras
Gibraltar
The Rock, Gibraltar Museum
Tarifa
Strait of Gibraltar
MOROCCO

N

0   10km
0   5 miles

○ ....City
◎ ....Large Town
○ ....Small Town
■ ....POI
▬ ....Motorway
— ....Main Road
— ....Minor Road
✈ ....Airport
▬ ....Railway

Gibralfaro: Either walk or take bus 35 or, by car, follow the signs from Plaza del General Torrijos. Open: 9am–9pm (closes 5.45pm in winter). Admission charge.

Catedral

Málaga's cathedral is low on architectural detail but big on imposing presence: it's the size of a small mountain. A hotchpotch of Gothic, Renaissance and Baroque, it is made odder by the absence of one of its towers (funds were diverted to Spain's war chest), which earned it the nickname La Manquita, the One-Armed Lady.
Calle Molina Lario. Open: Mon–Fri 10am–6pm, Sat 10am–5pm. Admission charge.

Museo Picasso

Picasso left Málaga when he was ten years old, but this hasn't deterred the city from celebrating him as if he had a lifelong attachment to his place of birth. The house where he was born and briefly lived (Casa Natal) on Plaza de la Merced has been turned into a gallery for exhibitions related to Picasso's work, but if you are at all curious about the man and his art you will want to make straight for the Museo Picasso in the former Palacio de Buenavista, which has a permanent collection of 155 works donated by the artist's daughter-in-law and grandson.
Calle San Agustín 8. Tel: 902 44 33 77. www.museopicassomalaga.org.

Open: Tue–Sun 10am–8pm (closes 9pm on Fri & Sat). Admission charge.

Antequera

The ancient town of Antequera has been a hub of Andalucía since before recorded time; today, it stands at the crossroads formed by motorways connecting Seville, Granada, Málaga and Córdoba, making it an easy place to get to from any direction.

If you want to tackle Antequera chronologically, start in the outskirts where there are three prehistoric dolmens of truly impressive size and construction.

The **Dolmen de Menga** (the oldest, built around 2500 BC) and the **Dolmen de Viera** stand together in an enclosure next to a petrol station. The **Dolmen de Romeral** is set apart, but it is worth visiting as well because it is built around an ingenious domed chamber.

The main cluster of monuments, however, all of relatively recent construction, is in the town centre and is reached via a street beside the tourist information office. The 16th-century **Arco de los Gigantes** (Giants' Arch) lets you into a square on which stands a Renaissance church. From here you have access to the Moorish fortress of the **Alcazaba**.
Dolmens: Open: Tue–Sat 9am–6pm, Sun 9.30am–2.30pm. Admission charge.
Alcazaba: Open: Tue–Fri 10.30am–2pm & 4–6pm, Sat 10.30am–2pm, Sun 11.30am–2pm, guided visits every half-hour. Free admission.

Historic Antequera climbs up a hillside

El Torcal

A group of rocks in the hills above Antequera has been shaped by the erosion of wind and water into a weird collection of natural sculptures. You can take one of two colour-coded routes to walk round El Torcal (now a nature reserve): the green route, *ruta verde* (1.5km/1 mile, allow 45 minutes), or the yellow route, *ruta amarilla* (3km/2 miles, allow 2 hours).
El Torcal Visitors' Centre. Tel: 952 70 25 05. Open: daily 10am–5pm.

Fuente de Piedra

The plains north of Antequera are somewhat dull, but a short way off the motorway towards Seville is Andalucía's largest natural lake which is home, in season, to a colony of flamingos. There's a visitors' centre beside the lake. You'll need a decent pair of binoculars.

Benalmádena

Many of Torremolinos's quieter tourist attractions, such as Sea Life and the Tivoli *parque temático* (theme park), are in this satellite town, which has a cable car going into the hills overlooking the town. Unusually, Benalmádena also has Europe's largest Buddhist *stupa* (temple) from which there are magnificent views over the coast.

Estepona

This is a fairly low-key resort with a big expat community, but still a working Spanish town. Away from the busy seafront, much of the town centre is pedestrian, with lateral boulevards and cobbled streets that run between two pleasant squares, Plaza las Flores and Plaza Arces. The town has a busy modernist Plaza de Toros, which hosts occasional concerts given by international artists touring Spain, and below it by the lighthouse a marina whose bars and clubs are less desperately trendy than those in Puerto Banús. Casares and the nearer Pueblos Blancos (*see pp72–81*) are a short drive or bus ride north.

Garganta del Chorro

Near Álora, the Río Guadalhorce squeezes through an impressive gorge known as the Garganta del Chorro. In 1921 King Alfonso XIII came here to inaugurate a dam, and, for his pleasure, a walkway of iron and concrete, the Caminito del Rey, was built on the walls of the gorge. Sadly, this splendid footpath is currently closed to the public for reasons of safety, with the slim chance that it will one day be restored. However, the gorge and a waterfall at the end of it can be admired from Restaurante El Pilar on the road towards Ardales. A detour off this road goes to the ruins of **Bobastro** where the horseshoe arches of the church built by a Mozarabic community (Christians living under Moorish rule) can still be seen.

The iconic Rock of Gibraltar

Gibraltar

Officially British, geographically part of Andalucía, and ethnically a mix of all the races that have ever passed through it, this small territory of disputed sovereignty is an anomaly in almost every sense, and for that it has its undeniable attractions. There is a quaint faux Britishness to the place, even if most of the English you hear will be delivered in an Andaluz accent.

A stroll along Gibraltar's central Main Street from Casemates Square to beyond the cathedral, with its preponderance of duty-free shops, fast-food outlets and British pubs, might have you assuming that this is nothing more than a shopping centre. Old Gibraltar hands, however, point out that there is another Gibraltar away from this shopping mall-cum-virtual casino, in its handsome old backstreets and squares.

Civil War

The causes of the Civil War that killed nearly half a million people in Spain between 1936 and 1939 can be traced back to the successive Carlist Wars of the 19th century and the failed attempts to introduce a democratic republic into this notoriously plutocratic society.

The loss of Spain's colonies in the 19th century undermined the economy, as did the phylloxera epidemic of the 1870s, which destroyed vineyards across Europe. Anarchists and others had been fomenting dissent throughout the second half of the 19th century, sparking strikes and occupations, usually put down brutally by the armed forces. By the start of the 20th century, Spain was already on the boil.

Spain's workers took to the nascent trade union movement at the turn of that century with a gusto unseen elsewhere in Europe. They formed rival political unions with vast memberships, some of which, such as the anarchist CNT, exist (in altered form) today. The first taste of what was to come broke out in Barcelona in 1909, during the *Setmana Tràgica* (tragic week), when a general strike turned into an uprising against the state and the Church, which the rioters saw as culpable in maintaining their misery.

Spain remained neutral during World War I, but with an economy spiralling into recession. Following what seems to have been a fairly common rule of 'When in doubt, stage a military coup', the powers that be appointed General Primo de Rivera, from Jerez, as head of its latest dictatorship. Rivera's regime survived until 1930.

Spain finally got a working republic in 1931, a coalition of anarchists, communists, socialists and liberals. This fractured alliance would be their

Málaga's Port Authority building was a key bomb target for fascist planes

Ronda's Puente Nuevo was used as a prison during the Civil War

fought on, most notably in Madrid, Barcelona and Málaga, for three years. The Republican struggle attracted support from overseas in the form of the International Brigades, who arrived in their hundreds from Britain, the USA and elsewhere. Madrid was one of the last cities to fall, in March 1939, and Franco declared a Nationalist victory in April.

Both sides committed terrible atrocities during the Civil War – Barcelona was the site of horrendous anti-clerical riots – and evidence of these, in particular mass revenge killings by Nationalists, is still being unearthed in the 21st century.

undoing, not least when the right-wing Falangists, formed in 1926, decided to take things into their hands. On 17 July 1936 General Franco led his garrison in Morocco in an open rebellion, airlifted his men to Seville, took the city and declared himself El Caudillo (The Leader). The Republicans, disorganised and riven by factional infighting, were no match for the 'Nationalists' and their allies in the Italian and German fascist movements, who aided El Caudillo with, for example, the blanket bombing of Gernika (Guernica).

Despite the superior firepower of the Nationalists, the Republicans

For decades there was agreement within Spain not to talk too much about the Civil War and its aftermath for fear of reopening the old divisions. Now, however, it is more openly discussed, although there are still two schools of thought. For latter-day apologists of the Nationalist cause, the military rebelled in order to reassert law and order in an increasingly destabilised country. But, given the longevity of Franco's subsequent dictatorship and its refusal to allow opposition voices to be heard, it is hard not to see the Civil War as a simple struggle between democracy and tyranny. Unfortunately for two generations of Spanish people, tyranny prevailed.

Visiting Gibraltar

Anyone from a country in the European Economic Area can visit Gibraltar by showing an identity card or a passport. All other nationals require a passport. Gibraltar trades in the Gibraltar pound, which is on a par with UK sterling. Most businesses in Gibraltar are also happy to accept euros.

For information on Gibraltar, *see www.gibraltar.gov.gi*

Getting there and around

Drivers are advised to park in Spain and walk across the border: delays are frequent and access is cut off whenever a flight lands on the runway of the small but busy airport between the border and the centre.

There are local and regional bus connections with La Línea de la Concepción, the town on the Spanish side of the border crossing, and bus or taxi links between the rail stations at either San Roque/La Línea or Algeciras.

The Rock

Inevitably, the Rock of Gibraltar is the most interesting part of the colony to visit. Unless you like hillwalking, the best policy is to take the cable car up and walk down. From the top station (which incorporates a restaurant) there are fabulous views over the town and harbour of Gibraltar, of Algeciras in Spain and, on a clear day, of the North African coast.

Much of the Rock is a nature reserve protected for its flora that includes two indigenous plants. And, of course, the Rock is inhabited by Barbary apes – in fact a species of tail-less monkey introduced by the British in the 18th century. These curious and mischievous creatures can snatch cameras and handbags and react aggressively when they feel threatened. Keep your distance, keep calm and they won't bother you.

From the cable-car top station, paths zigzag back down into town. Some 50km (31 miles) of tunnels have been carved into the Rock for military reasons and some sections are open to the public, such as the Great Siege Tunnels that were dug by the British army in 1779–83. They're only really worth visiting, though, if you are interested in military history.

Gibraltar Museum

Halfway along Main Street, along a lane to the right beyond the Cathedral of St Mary the Crowned, is the Gibraltar Museum. Its small but impressive display of artefacts ranges from the Moorish invasion of the Iberian peninsula up to its maritime exploits in recent centuries.
Gibraltar Museum: Bomb House Lane. www.gibmuseum.gi. Open: Mon–Fri 10am–6pm, Sat 10am–2pm. Admission charge.

Marbella

Marbella became a magnet for the jet set in the late 1950s and early 1960s, and established itself as perhaps the

A tiled bench in Marbella

most high-class resort on Spain's Mediterranean littoral. The intervening decades have been something of a roller-coaster ride for the resort and its smaller sibling, the marina playground of Puerto Banús, 4km (2½ miles) to the west (*see p94*).

Spain's laid-back attitude to international extradition treaties at this time also made it a haven for north European criminals and their booty – as well, alas, as their murderous feuds. Marbella's reputation nosedived after a series of particularly gruesome murders but it has since quietened down and reclaimed some of its earlier glamour.

Two men have left a particular legacy in modern-day Marbella: Prince Alfonso von Hohenlohe, an Austrian aristocrat who built the Marbella Club Hotel in the 1950s, and the former mayor, controversial business tycoon and boss of Atlético Madrid football club, Jesús Gil y Gil.

Marbella is an immensely attractive place to visit. It has a handsome seafront promenade, now lined with restaurants, and its lovely old Alameda, shaded by aged palms, gives on to a high-tech *rambla* (promenade) decorated with Salvador Dalí bronzes.

Casco antiguo (old town)

The *casco antiguo* (old town) has been exquisitely restored, nowhere more so than in Plaza de los Naranjos (Square of the Orange Trees), where the 17th-century *ayuntamiento* building overlooks some of the priciest bars in town. In fact, the whitewashed alleys and squares of the *casco* would give

Marbella's medieval fortifications

any of the Pueblos Blancos a run for their money.

The streets are full of handsome, well-kept buildings and interesting details, and half the fun is wandering around them without heading anywhere in particular. Highlights include the 16th-century Iglesia de la Encarnación, the pretty Plaza de Altamirano, the Renaissance Palacio Bazán and the walls of the old Arab castle.

Museo del Grabado Contemporáneo
Hidden in an alleyway behind the Iglesia de la Encarnación is the Museum of Contemporary Prints, housed in a Renaissance mansion originally built as a hospital. It has a sizeable collection of Mirós, some

smaller works by Picasso, and a feisty policy of showcasing contemporary art. The building itself, which comprises four floors, is worth the entry fee alone and is being expanded. The museum is close to the remnants of the Moorish ramparts.
Calle Hospital Bazán. Tel: 952 76 57 41. www.museodelgrabado.es. Open: Tue–Fri 9am–9pm, Sat & Mon 9am–2pm. Admission charge.

Mijas
Fuengirola on the coast is a package holiday resort and service centre, mainly useful for its train station; Mijas *pueblo*, a few kilometres behind it, is another story. A pretty old town now all but taken over by foreign residents, it is a nice place to escape from the beaches, apartment blocks and traffic for a stroll or a leisurely lunch.

Puerto Banús
This famous marina has long been a tourist attraction in its own right, although mainly for gawpers naively expecting a glimpse of celebrity millionaires. The boats are fun to look at (at any time, there must be half a billion euros moored in Puerto Banús), as are their owners, and there are numerous good, if expensive, seafood and American restaurants – and even an Indian one – on the quay. But Puerto Banús still has the slightly dislocated air of something that has just landed here from outer space.

Refugio de Juanar

If you need to escape from the coast for a while, this is one place to make for: a beauty spot high in the hills behind Marbella and Puerto Banús. To get there, take the road from Marbella to Ojén and follow the signs through pinewoods to a restaurant at the end of the road. Seven marked hiking trails radiate from here; the shortest one leads you 2.4km (1½ miles) to a viewpoint over the coast you have left behind.

San Pedro de Alcántara

Landlocked 1km (½ mile) away from its beach en route to Marbella, this is still a pleasant little Spanish town, with pedestrian streets and the handsome Plaza de la Iglesia where townsfolk promenade. It is also the main shopping centre for the booming *urbanizaciones*, gated housing developments, nearby, with multilingual bookshops and newsstands, restaurants and stores.

Torremolinos

Torremolinos is currently living down a reputation as a beer and beach resort, and the authorities are following Marbella's model in town gentrification, with replanted squares and pedestrian areas. It remains a big nightlife resort.

Western Costa del Sol

Inland, Mijas *pueblo* has a very different feel from its coastal counterpart

Eastern Costa del Sol

East of Málaga, the Costa del Sol is much less heavily developed than the Torremolinos–Estepona stretch, although the coast is filling up fast with new apartments and hotels, and the hills are being covered with private villas. The only major resorts along it are the relatively restrained Rincón de la Victoria, Torre del Mar and Nerja. Inland, however, is an entirely different story: the charming, hilly Axarquía is worth taking time to explore.

In common parlance, the whole of Spain's south coast is the Costa del Sol but officially it is a coast with three names. Beyond Nerja, the topography changes abruptly into the heavily indented and very attractive Costa Tropical, the coast of Granada province, thus named because of the orchards of tropical fruit that fill its valleys. This, in turn, changes its name 60km (40 miles) further on to the Costa de Almería, after the austere desert province that forms Spain's southeastern corner.

THE AXARQUÍA, THE COSTA TROPICAL AND NERJA
The Axarquía
The hills behind Vélez-Málaga and Nerja, a region called the Axarquía, are extremely picturesque and dotted with pretty villages. The convoluted contours mean that getting around here is slow and time-consuming; public transport is limited and a car is really the only way to see the sights. The colourful,

wine-producing town of **Cómpeta** is the de facto capital of upland Axarquía. In the valleys below it are two villages, **Archez** and **Salares**, in which the church towers are the undisguised Mudéjar brick minarets of mosques, dating from the 15th and 13th centuries respectively.

A separate journey takes you up a twisting road to **Comares**, a pretty town perched on a rocky peak from which there are prodigious views.

The Costa Tropical
The resorts of Granada province's coastline are mainly popular with Spanish holidaymakers, but they are gradually being discovered by foreign tourists and homeowners. The extension of the coastal motorway from Málaga and the completion of the motorway down the valley from Granada are likely to open them up further to the same internationalisation that has affected the Costa del Sol.

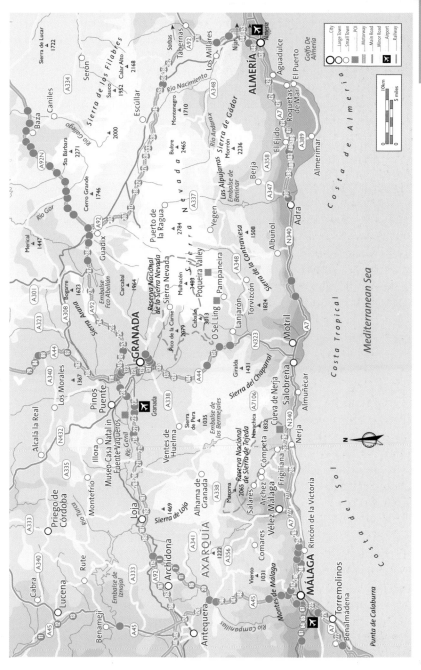

The two largest towns are the port of **Motril** and the resort of **Almuñécar**, founded by the Phoenicians, which sits under an Arab castle. In between them is **Salobreña**, which manages to be both a laid-back holiday resort and a typical Andalucian white town swarming over a great rock above the sea. There's a stiff walk up through the narrow streets to the castle, but you'll feel compensated for it by the view from the battlements.

The Costa Tropical's best beach is that contained by the horseshoe bay of **La Herradura** and checked in both directions by massive headlands beneath which are some of the best waters for scuba diving on the coast of Spain. The dive school in La Herradura's pretty harbour, Marina del Este, can take you on a brief tour of the seabed.

Nerja

Nerja is a growing, but still fairly low-rise, resort popular with foreign tourists, built around a viewing platform jutting over the Mediterranean (the Balcón de Europa). It has sparse historical or cultural interest, but outside the town is a cave – the **Cueva de Nerja**, styled as the 'Costa del Sol's natural cathedral' – which is used as the venue for an international festival of music and dance in the summer, and can be visited at other times. A short way inland from Nerja is the well-kept **Frigiliana**, certainly a contender for the prettiest town in Spain.

ALMERÍA PROVINCE

The easternmost province of Andalucía is a dry region that includes Europe's only desert. Its mountain ranges, ravines and badland landscapes can be stark and fascinating if you like to feel you are off the beaten track, but Almería has other attractions if you want them.

The first impression of Almería for many visitors, however, is not of unspoilt nature but of a sea of plastic sheeting. Warm winter temperatures here have encouraged farmers to turn their fields into vast greenhouses in order to supply northern European supermarkets with out-of-season vegetables.

The capital city, Almería, may not be high on anyone's must-see list, but it does have an impressive Alcazaba (castle) and the streets below are full of tapas bars. There are other sights scattered around the province, but above all it is the austere natural scenery that strikes the visitor. Sea and desert meet on the beautiful unspoilt beaches of the east coast, where you can escape the crowds.

Almería: the city

The least visited of Andalucía's regional capitals, this thriving port has much to recommend it to the visitor. It may lack the grand monuments of Seville and Granada, but there's plenty to explore, culture old and new, few of the crowds and hassles of the big cities, and a lively nightlife.

The aqueduct at Nerja

Almería, from the Arabic *al-mariya* (mirror of the sea), was a major port from the earliest days of the Moorish presence in Andalucía until their expulsion. City and region were severely damaged by an earthquake in 1522 and languished in poverty until the mid-20th century, when efforts began to revive agriculture and develop tourism. Despite the quake, some impressive sights remain, as do handsome examples of later architecture.

Alcazaba

This great Arab fortress is on three levels, with ongoing excavations, gardens and water courses and spectacular views all the way up to the Torre del Homenaje added by the Christian reconquerors of the city. From the second enclosure there are views over the **Centro Rescate de la Fauna Sahariana** (Centre for the Rescue of Saharan Fauna), a research centre where endangered gazelles from the western Sahara are bred.

Almería's old town from the sea

Almería's Alcazaba above the old town

Calle Almanzor. Open: Tue–Sun 9am–8.30pm (closes 6pm in winter). Admission charge; free to EU citizens.

Old Town

The old town between the Alcazaba, the Rambla de Beléi and the port boasts some very fine local architecture with a wealth of eccentric detail. Particularly recommended is **La Plaza Vieja**, also known as Plaza de la Constitución, on which stands the town hall clock.

If you don't care for monuments, come back at night when the old town is alive with bar hoppers: by tradition, each drink in Almería comes with a complimentary tapa.

Cable Inglés By far the most conspicuous of the city's monuments is a piece of industrial archaeology. The Cable Inglés is a great, hulking railway pier running briefly into the sea, which was built between 1902 and 1904 by a British company to load ore on to waiting ships.

Catedral Almería's cathedral sits in a stately square and shares its Gothic architecture, and architect Diego de Sileó, with the cathedral at Granada. The neo-primitive sun icon on its east (dawn-facing) wall has been read as evidence of freemasonry among 16th-century clergy, and is used as a logo by the city.
Plaza de la Catedral. Open: Mon–Fri 10am–4.30pm, Sat 10am–1pm. Admission charge.

Museo de Almería The province of Almería is rich in archaeology and this modern museum focuses on the two (*Cont. on p104*)

Walk: Cabo de Gata

Just over half an hour's drive or bus ride east of Almería city, Cabo de Gata is a dramatic volcanic headland and nature reserve that offers clean air, excellent views and unspoilt beaches. This walk begins at the fishing village and low-rise resort of San Miguel de Cabo de Gata. If you arrive by car you'll have to double back from the cape, but if you come by bus you can take another one back from San José at the end of an exhilarating hike that takes in some of Spain's finest coastal scenery.

Allow a whole day's walking (a good 6 hours) to get to the cape and back, or to reach San José (24km/15 miles). For bus information, ask at Almería bus station (*Plaza de la Estación. Tel: 950 26 20 98*) or contact **Autocares Bernardo** (*San José to Almería. Tel: 950 25 04 22. www.autocaresbernardo.com*).

1 San Miguel de Cabo de Gata

From the martello tower in San Miguel de Cabo de Gata head southeast (left facing the sea) towards the Salinas de Cabo de Gata.

2 Salinas de Cabo de Gata

These working salt pans, stretching between the town and Playa de la Fabriquilla, are a haven for indigenous and migratory birds, including, in season, flocks of flamingos and avocets, except in winter, when the pans are drained and harvested. Much of the salt industry is based here and at La Almadraba de Monteleva, 6km (4 miles) from the Cabo de Gata resort.

3 Playa de la Fabriquilla

At Playa de la Fabriquilla, the flat plains give way to the Sierra del Cabo de Gata hills, few of them above 400m (1,312ft) but dramatic in this setting.

The Cabo de Gata lighthouse

4 Faro de Cabo de Gata

The path (bike as well as foot) here joins the coast road and begins to rise up towards the cape itself, with its *faro* (lighthouse) perched on 200m (656ft)-high cliffs. There is an information point and magnificent *miradores* (viewing platforms), with varied views, a short stroll from the car park. At roughly 12km (7½ miles) from El Cabo de Gata resort, this is the spot to consider your options.

5 Mónsul and Los Genoveses

If you are going to continue rather than return to San Miguel de Cabo de Gata the way you came, follow the track beyond the lighthouse above the cliffs, which passes through a gate blocking the way to traffic. After the watchtower of La Vela Blanca you drop down to two beautiful beaches, the Playa de Mónsul (used in a key scene in the film *Indiana Jones and the Last Crusade*) and the Playa de los Genoveses, to reach the resort and principal settlement of the Cabo de Gata, San José.

6 San José

This expanding but still not oversized resort has ample hotels and restaurants, and makes a good place to stay for the night if you don't want to rush back to Almería.

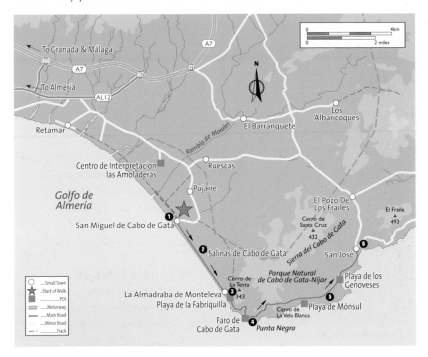

important prehistoric civilisations of Los Millares (*see page opposite*) and El Algar. The galleries are arranged around a hi-tech time-line column, which rises through three floors showing how remains are arranged in strata in the ground.

The exhibits are intended to bring the past alive for children, with TV screens and reconstructions.

If you are serious about your archaeology and don't have kids in tow, you'd be better off visiting the dig sites themselves. An annexe of the museum opposite the bus station has changing exhibitions of contemporary art.
Carretera de Ronda 91. Tel: 950 17 55 10. Open: Tue 2.30–8.30pm, Wed–Sat 9am–8.30pm, Sun 9am–2.30pm. Admission charge; free to EU citizens.

East coast

Very different in character is the coast northeast of Almería. In recent years, unchecked resort sprawl has made a mess of a beautiful line of beaches from **Carboneras** to beyond **Garrucha**, although some inaccessible coves have so far escaped the developers. The resort of **Mojácar** didn't escape this trend, but it still has a pretty town centre perched on a hill a little way inland. South of Carboneras, much of the coast has survived intact. The headland of **Cabo de Gata** is a nature reserve (*see pp102–3*).

Inland Almería

Tabernas is the most popular inland destination in Almería because of its Wild West theme parks, chief among

Almería's dusty interior

San José near Cabo de Gata is still relatively undeveloped

them **Mini-Hollywood**, which remain from the days when spaghetti Westerns were shot around here. Near it is an experimental solar power station, and not much further away is **Los Millares**, the excavated and partially restored settlement of a Copper Age civilisation.

Towards the coast is **Sorbas** and a hidden beauty spot and nature reserve of gypsum karst scenery. **Nijar**, in the hills between Sorbas and Cabo de Gata, is famed for its pottery. There are good views of Almería and its coast from the roads crossing two mountain ranges, the Sierra de los Filabres (passing by Calar Alto observatory) and the Sierra de Gádor (via Enix). The valley on the north side of Gádor leads into the Alpujarras (*see pp116–19*).

Mini-Hollywood: Carretera Nacional N340. Tel: 950 36 52 36. Open: Nov–Easter Sat & Sun 10am–7pm; Easter–May daily 10am–7pm; Jun–Oct daily 10am–9pm. Wild West shows at noon, 1pm, 3pm, 4pm & 5pm. Admission charge.

Los Millares: Santa Fé de Mondujar. Tel: 677 903 404. Open: Mon–Fri 8.30am–3pm, Sat 8.30am–1.30pm. Free admission.

South coast

Almería's southern coast is geographically an extension of the Costa del Sol and Costa Tropical, but much of it is unattractively swathed in the plastic greenhouses that have made many farmers millionaires, particularly around the boom town of El Ejido. The coast's main town is **Adra** and its biggest resorts are **Almerimar**, **Roquetas de Mar** and **Aguadulce**.

Undercover farming

For centuries until the late 20th century, the pattern of farming in Andalucía varied barely at all. The only crops grown were those adapted to the soil and climate; in accordance with agricultural know-how and available technology; and in response to demand from local markets.

Thus, some parts of the region have come to specialise in a particular produce – the wetlands at the mouth of the Guadalquivir grow rice; the hills of Jaén supply olives for olive oil; and the coast of Granada has a microclimate suitable for growing subtropical fruits.

Much of the land in Andalucía, however, is too dry to be of much use other, perhaps, than for grazing goats. Almería province in the east, in particular, has such a low rainfall that generation after generation of its youth had to emigrate in search of work elsewhere. Then, in the 1970s, an agricultural revolution began that would not only create unprecedented numbers of jobs but make some farmers millionaires.

The stimulus was the increasingly insatiable demand of supermarket shoppers in the north of Europe for what they wanted to eat when they wanted. Almería may have little rainfall, it was realised, but it more than made up for this in winter sunshine, and if this could be managed to cheat the seasons fruits and vegetables could be made to crop early to meet the whims of British, German, Scandinavian and Benelux consumers for year-round tomatoes, lettuces and strawberries.

Rapidly, vast tracts of Almería were turned into extensive seas of polythene sheeting: greenhouses in which growing conditions could be controlled by means of drip-feeding systems, fertilisers and pesticides. The only commodity needed from nature was the warmth of the sun which boosted temperatures inside the polytunnels by a vital few degrees above the air outside.

The effects of this new method of farming were spectacular. The flow of labour was reversed and Almería now began to attract migrants of its own. Fortunes were made by those farmers who could muster the investment necessary for this new kind of intensive agriculture and do the deals to sell their crops.

The nondescript village of El Ejido grew into the capital of this plastic

Inside a pepper greenhouse

agriculture and was transformed from a one-horse town to the haunt of bankers and venture capitalists. Today, it is an odd mixture of warehouses stocked with pipes, seeds and tools, and luxury shops where newly rich farmers can spend their profits.

The plastic revolution has subsequently crept along the coast from Almería and is now estimated to cover an area equivalent to the island of Ibiza. Despite the employment it creates, not everyone is in favour of it. Visually, it is hard to describe it as anything other than a blight on the landscape and some towns have resisted its invasion, hoping that tourism will make up for the jobs being turned away.

Environmentalists, meanwhile, consider it an eco-disaster in the making. The residues of all those chemicals have to go somewhere. And plastic does not last forever: it disintegrates and gets scattered by the wind leaving an unsightly mess.

Recently, there has been talk that the agricultural revolution is coming to an end. North Africa is now trying to pull off the same trick as Almería, only with the advantage of much cheaper labour costs. It could be that, in the end, Andalucía's traditional farming practices prove more sustainable in all senses.

Granada and Sierra Nevada

As the Christian Reconquest of Spain proceeded, one anachronistic Muslim kingdom, Granada, was left functioning until 1492. A late flowering of Moorish civilisation produced the Alhambra, one of the most exquisite buildings in the world. Granada's defeated and exiled Moors initially took refuge in the picturesque valleys on the other side of Spain's highest mountain range, the Sierra Nevada.

GRANADA

Dominated by the sprawling Alhambra but with a wealth of other monuments within easy walking distance of the base of the Alhambra hill, Granada is an ideal city for strollers. It's barely one-third the size of Seville, with a similar population ratio, but has a culture to rival that of its larger sibling. Granada's sights are concentrated in three areas: the hill of the Alhambra (*see below*), the facing hill of the Albaicín (*see pp114–15*) and the city centre around the cathedral.

The Alhambra

The oldest parts of the Alhambra, notably the Alcazaba (fortress), date from the 9th century, and later additions up to the 14th century.

The Alhambra takes its name from the Arabic *Al Qal'a al-Hamra* (red fort), from the red-coloured walls of its earliest structures. Little of the earliest fortress remains, and it was rebuilt in the 11th century and again in the 13th

by the Nasrid rulers who were to build the **Palacios Nazaríes**.

The Alcazaba is one of three groups of monuments here, along with the Casas Reales, which include the Palacios, and the adjoining Generalife gardens. At its peak in the 14th century, the Alhambra comprised an entire royal city in miniature.

Ownership changed abruptly after the long winter of 1491–2, when Isabel and Fernando with an army of 150,000 laid siege to this last bastion of Moorish rule, defeating Boabdil in January 1492.

Alcazaba

Much of the original fort is ruined, but some vestiges remain, most notably the **Torre de la Vela** bell tower, named after the bell that used to be rung to mark the hours when the irrigation system watered Granada's Vega, or agricultural plain. The Christian flag was first flown from this battlement on 2 January 1492 to announce the city's capture.

Casas Reales

Across the **Plaza de los Aljibes** (cisterns) is the entry to the Palacios, down a ramp or stairs. This is the area of the Alhambra where you will be allotted a half-hour window to enter – miss it and you'll have to come back another day or buy another ticket. The Palacios are all built around water, light and open spaces. Traffic through them, especially if you get caught between the combat-ready hordes that roam the complex led by their commando-like guides, is slow and one-way.

Harén The centre of the Serrallo, where the *harén* (harem) occupants would recline, is also the archetypal

Granada (*see pp114–15 for walk route*)

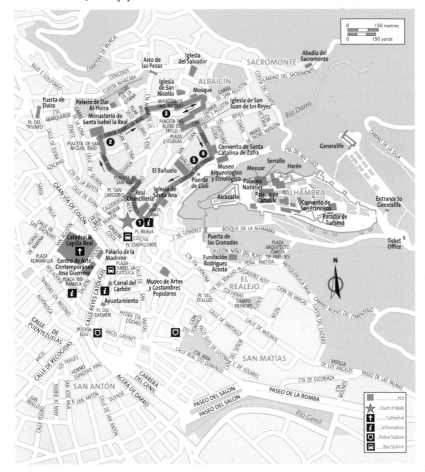

feature of the Alhambra: the **Patio de los Leones**, with its twelve lions supporting a fountain at the centre of symmetrical watercourses, overlooked by delicate arcading.

The neighbouring **Sala de los Abencerrajes**, named after the family of a rival of Boabdil supposedly slaughtered at a banquet here, has the most impressive ceiling of the entire Alhambra. Its fantastical stucco patterns are based on Pythagoras' famed theorem about the properties of the right-angled triangle.

Mexuar The first section of the Palacios is a council chamber built around a courtyard in 1365 where the sultan would consult with his viziers and also hear petitions for mercy or favour from his subjects. It leads on through the **Patio del Cuarto Dorado** (Gold Quarter) to the first of the Palacios' marvels, the Serrallo, or harem.

The Alhambra's masterpiece, the Patio de los Leones

Serrallo The palace that housed the sultan's wives is approached through the cool rectangular space of the **Patio de Arrayanes**, named after the trimmed myrtles that hedge its placid pond. As well as the rooms giving on to the arcaded spaces around the pool, this is dominated by the **Salón de Embajadores** (Hall of the Ambassadors), where sensitive matters of state were dealt with and where Boabdil negotiated his surrender in 1492. The Salón has a magnificent latticed wood ceiling, whose criss-crossed knot-like patterns represent the seven heavens of Moorish cosmology.

Palacio de Carlos V The exit from the Palacios leads into this later, Christian addition to the complex, built in the 16th century by the eponymous king. This Renaissance palace was never finished, but now serves as the **Museo de la Alhambra** (*open: Tue–Sat 9am–2pm. Admission charge; free to EU citizens*) which has an excellent collection of Spanish–Moorish artefacts.

Convento de San Francisco Behind the Palacio are the remains of the original royal city, including its convent, nowadays serving as Granada's overpriced *parador* hotel, which is often booked up months in advance. The bar and restaurant are open to non-residents, and the garden is a great place to drink in the view.

The Palacio del Partal, the oldest remnant of the fort

Generalife

The neighbouring gardens, translated variously from the Arabic *Yannat al Arif* as 'gardens of the architect' or 'lofty paradise', were begun in the 13th century and originally included orchards and pasture. Later designs transformed them into a maze of exquisite watercourses and topiary ideal for romantic intrigues.

Planning your visit

The Alhambra is reached from Plaza Nueva by car, by the special Alhambra bus service or on foot (20 mins) up the steep wooded Cuesta (Hill) de Gomérez. There's a large car park by the entrance, which is to your left.

The authorities reckon the average visitor needs three hours to visit the Alhambra, which is a conservative estimate. Whatever time you decide to visit your ticket will be stamped with a half-hour window (usually an hour or more in advance) during which you must enter the Palacios Nazaríes area, although once past the entrance you can stay as long as you like. You should thus plan your route through the Alhambra around this.

There are toilets and refreshments (sometimes just vending machines) at various points around the complex, and you should bear in mind that much of the site is out in the open (take hats and sunblock). There is wheelchair

The exquisite Patio de la Acequia in the Generalife gardens

access, but not to every nook and cranny, and parts can be very crowded. *Alhambra and Generalife. www.alhambra-patronato.es. Open: mid-Mar–mid-Oct Sun–Thur 8.30am–8pm, Fri–Sat 8.30am–9.30pm; mid-Oct–mid-Mar Sun–Thur 8.30am–6pm, Fri–Sat 8.30am–6pm & 10–11.30pm. Box office closes one hour earlier. To avoid queues and disappointment, it's better to buy entrance tickets in advance. Tickets can be purchased by credit card at La Caixa bank, by telephone (Tel: 902 88 80 01), or online (www.alhambra-tickets.es). Admission charge.*

El Bañuelo

These exquisite Arab baths were built in the 11th century and thus predate the finest parts of the Alhambra.
Carrera del Darro 31. Tel: 958 02 78 00. Open: Tue–Sat 10am–2pm. Free admission.

Catedral and Capilla Real

Granada's mountainous cathedral, begun by Diego de Siloé in the 16th century but only completed in the 18th, is, despite its size, decidedly modest in its interior. Light and airy, thanks to its 27m (88½ft)-high dome, its various chapels feature sculptures by Alonso Cano and an El Greco portrait of St Francis.

Of greater interest is its neighbouring Capilla Real, built as a mausoleum for the *Reyes Católicos*, Isabel and Fernando, as well as their daughter Juana, 'La Loca' (The Mad), and her husband Felipe, 'El Hermoso' (The Handsome). There is, however, doubt whether these are the true remains of Isabel and Fernando, as their original graves in the Alhambra had been defiled before the contents were moved to the Capilla.
Gran Vía de Colón. Catedral open: Mon–Sat 10am–1.30pm & 4–8pm, Sun 4–8pm (closes at 7pm in winter). Admission charge. Capilla Real open: summer Mon–Sat 10.30am–1.30pm & 4–7pm, Sun 11am–1pm & 4–7pm; winter Mon–Sat 10.30am–1pm & 3.30–6.30pm, Sun 11am–1pm & 3.30–6.30pm. Admission charge.

Corral del Carbón

An Arab *caravanserai* – inn and warehouse for merchandise – adapted by the Christian *renconqueros* (independent missionaries) for use as a theatre.
Mariana Pineda. Tel: 958 22 59 90. Open: Mon–Fri 10.30am–1.30pm & 5–8pm, Sat 10.30am–2pm. Free admission.

Plaza Bib-Rambla

A few short blocks from the corner of Gran Vía de Colón and Calle Reyes Católicos, south of Plaza Nueva, this is the nearest this oddly de-centred city has to a focal point. The pretty square is lined with bars and restaurants, handy for the cathedral.

Plaza Nueva

This large space is dominated by the **Real Chancillería**, built in the 16th century to house law courts, and the **Iglesia de Santa Ana**. From the top end of the square the Carrera del Darro follows the river of the same name towards the Sacromonte cave and gypsy quarter. Along it or just off it are several important buildings. Behind the Chancillería, alleys slope steeply up into the Albaicín, but a more comfortable way to get there is to take Calle Calderería Vieja, which starts just around the corner from Plaza Nueva, on Calle de Elvira. From the bottom of the square it is a short distance to the Plaza de Isabel la Católica at the end of the Gran Vía de Colón, Granada's main street.

Here and around Plaza Nueva and the Albaicín are the best places to hunt for a meal, drink or entertainment. The large student population and a lively lesbian/gay community guarantee a plethora of trendy hangouts.

Granada and Sierra Nevada

The red fort in winter with the snows of the Sierra Nevada in the distance

Walk: The Albaicín

The hill opposite the Alhambra is occupied by the Albaicín, the most perfectly preserved Moorish quarter in Andalucía. Most of the streets are narrow and stepped, meaning that you'll meet few cars to bother you. The characteristic house of the Albaicín is the carmen, *a villa concealed behind high walls. You can get up to the viewpoint at the top of the Albaicín and back in an hour, but for a leisurely stroll allow two hours.* See map on p109.

1 Plaza Nueva

The walk begins in this busy square, on a corner of which, beside the **Iglesia de Santa Ana**, stands the tourist office. Plaza Nueva is dominated by the **Real Chancillería**, the Royal Chancellery, designed by Diego de Siloé and completed in 1530.

2 Placeta de San Miguel Bajo

Take Cárcel Alta, the street to the left of the Chancellery as you look at it. Turn left at the top and turn sharp right in the cobbled square of Plaza San Gregorio. Almost immediately turn off left heading steeply uphill on Calle San José. Ahead of you is the lovely 10th-century minaret of San José. Go uphill underneath this, passing the handsome doorway of the Carmen San Luís. Continue uphill into Placeta de San Miguel Bajo, dominated by a whitewashed church. Note the 13th-century Moorish cistern in the corner of the square.

3 Mirador de San Nicolás

Follow the straight Calle Santa Isabel la Real along the hill past the 16th- to 17th-century monastery towards your next goal, the white church tower of **San Nicolás**. At the point where the road starts to head downhill, turn left then right, and you'll end up in the square known as the Mirador de San Nicolás, famed for its view of the Alhambra directly across the Darro valley. Note that there will be more views of the Alhambra on the way down.

4 Down to the Río Darro

Leave the square on the road that runs along the bottom of it, the Cuesta de las Cabras, which is short-stepped and steep. On your way down you pass Granada's **mosque** on the left. Turn right and right again and you come to a dog-leg; continue downhill via the Placeta del Comino. On your left is the 15th-century Carmen de Aben Humeya. This road reverts to steps to reach an irregularly shaped square, the Placeta del Aljibe de Trillo, named after a 14th-century cistern (on your right). Turn left at the bottom of the square on Azacayuela de San Pedro, down some steps and round a sharp corner. Turn right at the next junction along the slope to reach Plaza Escuelas, on which stands the **Iglesia de San Juan de los Reyes**. Cross the road into Calle Zafra, a straight street which brings you out on the road that runs beside the Darro, next to the **Museo Arqueológico y Etnológico** in the Casa de Castril (*open: Tue 2.30–8pm, Wed–Sat 9am–8.30pm, Sun 9am–2.30pm. Admission charge; but free to EU citizens*) and opposite the church.

5 Along the river

Turn right and almost immediately you pass the open door of the 16th-century **Convento de Santa Catalina de Zafra**, where invisible nuns sell cakes via a turntable. There is a ruined half-arch (Moorish) hovering above the river to the left. Soon you will pass the 11th-century Moorish baths of **El Bañuelo**, whose vaulted interiors are illuminated by star-shaped skylights.

Plaza Nueva, your starting point, is now ahead of you. If you want a quieter stroll, take one of the two bridges across the river and turn right, which will bring you to the tourist office.

View of the Albaicín from the Alhambra

Walk: The Albaicín

AROUND GRANADA

There are a few sights in the province that justify an excursion. Chief among them are **Las Alpujarras** (*see below*), the towns of **Montefrío** and **Alhama de Granada** and the troglodyte quarter of **Guadix**. And if you have any interest in literature, you can go in search of Spain's most famous poet, Federico García Lorca.

Alhama de Granada

It takes a long drive from Granada city through rolling farmland to get to this town on the lip of a gorge. Its main draw is inside the spa-hotel at the end of a smaller gorge below the town. Here guests can use delightful 12th-century Moorish baths. Non-residents can visit them every afternoon from 2pm to 4pm. Alternatively, you can just sit in the river outside the hotel and bathe for free in the naturally heated waters.

54km (33 miles) southwest of Granada.

Las Alpujarras

These deep and steep mountain valleys south of Granada compose one of the most geographically and culturally distinct regions of Andalucía. Their remote villages became natural refuges for Moors fleeing the Christian conquerors after the Reconquest.

Their natural charm and lingering sense of tradition have made them a natural bolt-hole for people seeking a peaceful rural life. For the past three or so decades, the Alpujarras have increasingly become home to northern European dropouts and downsizers whose presence has probably helped sustain mountain villages which might otherwise have been abandoned, as has happened elsewhere in Andalucía. The most celebrated of these new arrivals is Chris Stewart, whose books *Driving Over Lemons, A Parrot in the Pepper Tree* and *The Almond Blossom Appreciation Society* have made the town of Órgiva and its environs world famous.

There's only one twisting road through the scenic part of the Alpujarras, with spurs to any villages not directly on it, so you won't get lost. The downside is that you'll have to double back to return to your starting point or make a lengthy loop, curving around endless mountainsides. To start a tour, take the motorway from Granada towards the coast and turn off for the spa town of Lanjarón. Just before Órgiva, the main market town of the western Alpujarras, a road ascends towards the High Alpujarras. There is a bus service to the main villages of the Alpujarras from Granada. In recent years a number of comfortable and charming hotels have opened in the Alpujarras, making this a good place to escape if you are in need of peace and fresh air.

The Alpujarras continue into the neighbouring province of Almería but the scenery is less beautiful and the villages generally less interesting.

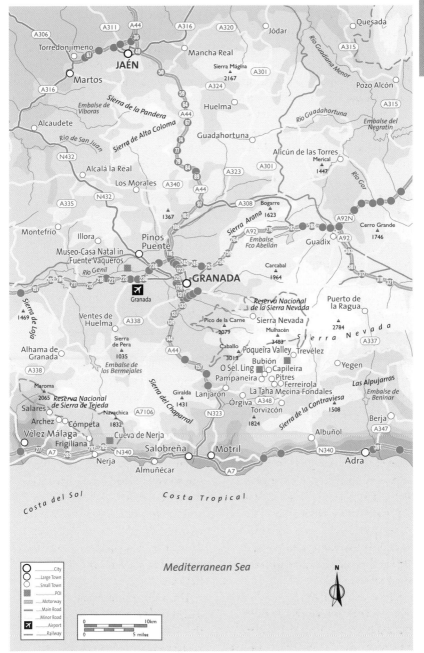

Map labels:

A306, A311, A44, A316, A320, Jódar, Quesada

Torredonjimeno, 36, 40, A315, Mancha Real

JAÉN, 50, Sierra Mágina 2167, A301, Pozo Alcón

Martos, A324, A316, 59, 64, Huelma, A315, Río Guadiana Menor

Embalse de Viboras, Sierra de la Pandera, A44, 67, Río Guadahortuna, Embalse del Negratín

Alcaudete, Sierra de Alta Coloma, 74, Guadahortuna

Río de San Juan, 77, Alicún de las Torres, Merical 1447

N432, 79, 84, A323, A301, Río Gor

Alcalá la Real, 89, A340, A44

Los Morales, A335, N432, 97, A308, Bogarre, A92N, Cerro Grande 1746

Montefrío, 1367, 103, Sierra Arana 1623, A92, Guadix, A92

Illora, 108, Embalse Fco Abellán, A92

Pinos Puente, 116, 155, 303

Museo-Casa Natal in Fuente Vaqueros, 236, 245, 249, 252, 256, Carcabal 1964

Río Genil, 123, 126, GRANADA

203, 206, 219, 221, 225, 230, 126

191, 212, 216, 131, Granada ✈, 135

Ventes de Huelma, A338, 139, Pico de la Carne 2079, Sierra Nevada, Puerto de la Ragua, 2784

Sierra de Loja 1469, Sierra de Pera 1035, 144, Mulhacén 3483, Sierra Nevada, A337

Alhama de Granada, A44, Caballo 3013, Poqueira Valley, Trevélez

A338, Embalse de los Bermejales, 157, O Sél. Ling, Bubión, Capileira, Yegen

Maroma 2065, Reserva Nacional de Sierra de Tejeda, Giralda 1431, Pampaneira, Pitres, Ferreirola, Las Alpujarras

Salares, Navachica, Lanjarón, La Taha Mecina-Fondales, Embalse de Beninar

Archez, Cómpeta 1832, A7106, Órgiva, A348, Sierra de la Contraviesa, Berja

Vélez Málaga, Sierra del Chaparral, N323, Torvizcón 1508, A347

Frigiliana, Cueva de Nerja, Salobreña, Albuñol

A7, 297, 295, N340, Motril, N340, Adra, 391

Nerja, Almuñécar, A7

Costa del Sol, Costa Tropical

Mediterranean Sea

N

Legend:
- City
- Large Town
- Small Town
- POI
- Motorway
- Main Road
- Minor Road
- ✈ Airport
- Railway

0 ——— 10km
0 ——— 5 miles

The spa town of Lanjarón, source of Spain's most popular bottled water

After Granada fell to the Christians in 1492 (the same year Columbus sailed), the last Moorish king, Boabdil, was 'given' the Alpujarras as his personal fiefdom. The pass south of Granada where he is said to have paused for a last glimpse of his fallen kingdom is known as Puerto del Suspiro del Moro (Gate of the Moor's Sigh). It was only a year, however, until Boabdil was sent into exile in North Africa. Following a doomed uprising in the Alpujarras, the final Mudéjars, those 'allowed to stay', were either expelled or forcibly converted. Two Moorish households were kept in each village to help maintain the agricultural system but otherwise the Alpujarras were repopulated by Christian settlers from northern Spain.

One of the most appealing aspects of the Alpujarras is the vernacular architecture that echoes the Berber buildings of North Africa. The typical house of the Alpujarras is built of stone and has a flat roof spread with an impermeable layer of gravel, from which sprouts a tall, capped chimney. The villages are complicated clusters of such houses, each stuck to its neighbours, with erratic narrow, stepped and tapering streets squeezing between them.

Fuente Vaqueros

One of the first victims in the Spanish Civil War was the *granadino* poet Federico García Lorca, shot in an olive grove outside the town of Víznar.

GERALD BRENAN

Before Chris Stewart, it was another writer, Gerald Brenan, who put the Alpujarras on the map. He sought refuge in the village of Yegen for a number of years after World War I and wrote about his experiences in the classic book *South from Granada*.

In Brenan's time the Alpujarras were still extremely remote and little developed, and he was able to record traditional life before modernity began to arrive. There is nothing to see in Yegen marking Brenan's stay except a plaque on the wall of the house in which he lived.

There's a museum-shrine to Lorca at the Huerta de San Vicente on the outskirts of Granada city, but the best place to go to find out about him, his work, his friends and his short life is the house where he was born, **Museo-Casa Natal** in Fuente Vaqueros. *19km (12 miles) northwest of Granada. Museo-Casa Natal Federico García Lorca: Calle Poeta García Lorca. Tel: 958 51 64 53. www.museogarcialorca.org. Open for guided visits only: Jul–Aug Tue–Sun 10am, 11am, noon & 1pm; Oct–Mar Tue–Sun 10am, 11am, noon, 1pm, 4pm & 5pm; Apr–Jun & Sept Tue–Sun 10am, 11am, noon, 1pm, 5pm & 6pm. Admission charge.*

Guadix

One of the most remarkable urban sights in the whole of Andalucía is the lumpy sandstone landscape around Guadix. The hills first appear at neighbouring Purullena, as do the

The pretty village of Trevélez is renowned for its dry-cured hams

tell-tale television aerials jutting from the ground. In Purullena, like its neighbour, many people live underground (an estimated 10,000 of them in Guadix), in modernised cave dwellings. Several caves have been converted into luxury hotels.

The cave district of Guadix is an easy walk or drive signposted from the centre, which also boasts an impressive sandstone cathedral by de Siloé and an attractive *casco antiguo*. There's a good museum at the heart of the district.

55km (34 miles) northeast of Granada. Cueva Museo: Plaza Ermita Nueva. Tel: 958 66 08 08. Open: Mon–Sat 10am–2pm & 5–7pm, Sun 10am–2pm. Admission charge.

The High Alpujarras

Lanjarón

Famed throughout Spain as the source of the bottled spring water sold in every Spanish supermarket, Lanjarón has been a centre of population and a renowned spa since Roman times. The *balneario*, or spa, is on its one main street, Avenida Andalucía, and in summer months throngs with people.

Montefrío

Built on a steep slope and surrounded by olive trees, Montefrío has two interesting churches, the perfectly circular **Iglesia de la Encarnación** and the 16th-century Gothic **Iglesia de la Villa**. The latter contains a museum, the **Centro de Interpretación La**

Centinela, exploring the conflicts between Moors and Christians. *52km (32 miles) northwest of Granada. Centro de Interpretación La Centinela open: times vary. Check with Tourist Information Office; Tel: 958 33 60 04.*

O Sel. Ling

On the way up to the High Alpujarras there is a turning from a mountain pass to this Tibetan Buddhist retreat centre, but you will need to follow a minor road and then a track for 7km (4½ miles). It is open to visitors except during retreats. *www.oseling.com*

Poqueira Valley

By far the most attractive part of the Alpujarras – and the most popular – is the higher part of the **Barranco de** **Poqueira** (Poqueira Valley). Here there are three villages; the lowest of them, through which the road passes first, is **Pampaneira**. As you continue to climb past it you will get a good view of the flat-roofed houses and their idiosyncratic chimneys.

Bubión and **Capileira** are reached by a detour from the main road. Both are attractive places to take a stroll and make good bases for a few days' walking. Beyond Capileira the road continues towards the summits of the Sierra Nevada, and you can take a minibus excursion from the Sierra Nevada National Park visitors' centre to the peaks above.

La Taha

Round another few corners from the Poqueira Valley is another group of

Montefrío in the high Alpujarras

villages known collectively as La Taha. The two prettiest are down the slope, **Mecina Fondales** and **Ferreirola**. Pitres is a larger town on the main road.

Trevélez

Spain's highest village (at 1,476m/ 4,843ft) uses its altitude to dry-cure hams that are renowned throughout Andalucía. From here the scenery of the Alpujarras becomes less attractive and the villages less interesting, so this is a good place to turn around if you don't want to do a lot more driving.

If you want to make a circular tour of the Alpujarras, continue past Trevélez and take one of the next two turnings right (south), either of which will bring you to the small wine-producing town of Torvizcón and thus back to Órgiva and the road out of the Alpujarras via

Thousands of *granadinos* take to the slopes on winter weekends

Lanjarón. A much longer route is to continue on the main road towards Almería and cross the Sierra Nevada by the Puerto de la Ragua pass, which brings you on to a motorway back to Granada.

Skiing in the Sierra Nevada

Just 31km (19 miles) and 45 minutes' drive southeast of Granada is Europe's southernmost ski resort, with a season running from December until April. It has staged various winter sports tournaments, is a major snowboarding centre and also boasts that it has the most sunshine of any European ski resort.

The Sierra Nevada ski station has over 50 different marked runs in seven different areas of the mountain, at altitudes roughly between 2,000m (6,562ft) and 3,000m (9,842ft) above sea level. These range from easy to very difficult, but also include training slopes and areas dedicated to non-skiing pastimes including snowbiking, sledging, luge and tobogganing.

There is also a wide range of accommodation, from youth hostels to smart four-star hotels, as well as restaurants, bars, banks, boutiques and even a cinema. Most of these open for the ski season, although some restaurants, bars and shops (but not hotels) open to serve summer trade, as well as during the run-up and close-down at either end of the season. The *granadinos* who have made it so popular tend to head straight for the piste, and it should be pointed out that Sierra Nevada is no Gstaadt: its bars, cafés and boutiques might more accurately be compared with a large motorway service station.

Ecologists take a dim view of the ski station, particularly in such an area as the Sierra Nevada, although the resort claims to be pursuing an ecologically sensitive policy. The environmental impact of thousands of visitors a day, however, intent on skiing to the extent that the resort has one of the largest hi-tech snow-making systems in Europe, deploying hundreds of 'cannons' and 'guns' to fire instant piste on to the slopes, has to be considerable.

Non-skiers and sightseers are allowed on to three of the transport systems around the slopes, the Parador chairlift and the Al-Andalus and Borreguiles cable cars, which include round-trip rides up to the higher slopes. The ski station (Estación de Esqui) itself, where dozens of *taquillas* (ticket windows) open to deal with the hordes who descend when ski conditions are good, also hires out a complete range of clothing and gear, as do some hotels (including the youth hostels). Equally, however, the resort welcomes those who just want to lark about on dustbin-lid-style plastic sledges. There are also routes for dog-sledging and horse-drawn sleighs, snowmobiling and inflatable toboggans. Away from the slopes, there is also an astronomy programme and there are hiking routes around the resort.

Walk: Sierra Nevada

This is a short mountain walk for the summer months, with optional detours or cut-offs along the way. It is circular, with an average round-trip time of five hours, less if you opt for some of the swifter return routes. It shifts between paths, tracks and roads. At this altitude (above 2,000m/6,562ft, rising to over 3,000m/9,842ft) the usual warnings about wearing firm footwear and protective clothing and taking adequate supplies and sunburn precautions need to be stressed.

A shorter winter option still is to make the walk circular but with Estación de Borreguiles as the destination, either by taking the road and path up and the ski lift down, or vice versa.

Heading up above the snow line

The walk can be begun either from Pradollano, which has public transport connections, or in the vicinity of the Albergue Universitario, the youth hostel used by students from Granada and elsewhere during study trips.

1 Ski resort

There are two options from Sierra Nevada ski resort to Borreguiles, either the conventional walk described below or a quicker cheat's walk using the ski lift (not operating in summer). The second route is also an option if you just want to walk part of the way, say, to the astronomical observatory, and turn back.

2 Albergue Universitario

If you decide to walk, take the A395 mountain road from the middle of the ski resort up to the Albergue. Here take the path signposted off to the right heading for the Virgen de las Nieves area, one of the numerous parascending (*parapente*) spots here.

This leads to the Cruce (crossroads) de Borreguiles, where the path forks left and right, the former following the road on up.

3 Estación de Borreguiles

The right-hand path strikes off into open country and towards the Estación de Borreguiles ski-lift station. Above the station to the west is the IRAM radio telescope station, one of three observatories this route passes.

4 Embalse de las Yeguas

From Borreguiles, the route continues up in a fairly straightforward fashion until reaching the second observatory, above a T-junction where another path joins this route from the west (your right). Continue straight on until you reach the Embalse de las Yeguas, a small lake-like reservoir, and a series of smaller lakelets beyond.

Here another T-junction leads left and right: take the left fork, heading back towards the road at Carihuela.

5 Carihuela

At Carihuela, there are various options. You are within striking distance of the peak of El Veleta, second in height only to its neighbour, Mulhacén, mainland Spain's highest peak. Several other high-ridge walks leave here, including a circular route via Garro del Caballo, and an even longer march over the peaks to Capileira (*see p121*). However, these are beyond the reach of the day walker,

and anyone without serious gear and experience.

The simplest route back to Pradollano or the Albergue is by the (blocked) road as it zigzags back down, or the quicker but rougher route as the track cuts across the meanders of the road down to Cruce de Borreguiles. The path continues to short-cut across the road's turns, passing under the third observatory seen on this route, down to the Albergue.

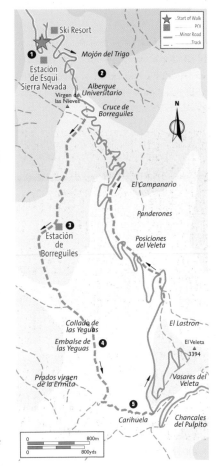

Northern Andalucía

Andalucía's two northernmost provinces, Jaén and Córdoba, run up to the Sierra Morena mountain range which is almost impassable with very few roads across it, the main one being the dramatic gorge of the Desfiladero de Despeñaperros. They are joined by the River Guadalquivir, flowing west, and an undulating swarm of olive trees producing high-quality olive oils. Prime places to visit here are the wooded sierras of Cazorla, the Renaissance towns of Úbeda and Baeza, and the city of Córdoba.

JAÉN PROVINCE
Jaén

Probably the least prepossessing city in Andalucía, Jaén nevertheless has a number of attractions worth a detour and makes an excellent base or overnight stop for exploring the region. Its Santa Catalina castle (best viewed at twilight arriving from Granada) has one of the most dramatic sites in the whole of Spain.

A centre of olive production since Roman times and earlier (archaeological finds have established links with Greek sea traders), Jaén city and province have been dominated by the doughty *Olea europea* (European olive) for millennia. A key post in Moorish *al-Andalus*, it was recaptured by Fernando III's armies in 1246 and entered an economic decline that only saw an upswing in the past century.

In the town, particularly in the *casco antiguo* behind the monumental cathedral, there are some fascinating sights. Jaén is also a university town, with a separate art school, and a student culture to match.

Baños Árabes

The most important sight after the castle and cathedral is the Arab baths, which are among the finest preserved examples in Spain, and form one of three museums now housed in a 16th-century palace that was deliberately built over the remains.

The baths themselves were built on what were probably the remains of earlier Roman baths, taking advantage of hot-water springs that suggest volcanic activity in the region. A glass floor has been placed over the central sections so that visitors walk over the remains as though through the air. Above the baths, on the ground floor and upper levels of the 16th-century **Palacio de Villadompardo**, is the **ethnological museum**, dedicated to the olive industry and domestic customs over the centuries. The ethnological museum shares its upper floor with

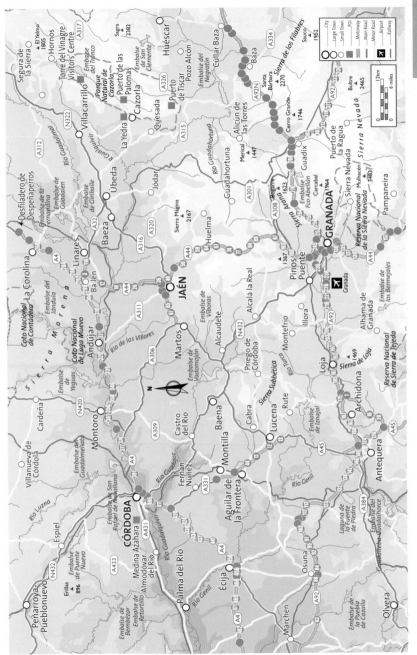

the curious **Museo Internacional de Arte Naïf**, a collection of largely Spanish naive art. A lower gallery is also dedicated to contemporary artworks.

Calle Martínez Molina. Open: Tue–Sat 8.45am–9.30pm, Sun 9.15am–2.45pm. Free admission.

Castillo de Santa Catalina

Jaén's spectacular castle looms high above the city on a rocky pinnacle that takes an hour and a half to reach on foot. The fortress was built by the Moors over an existing tower which was believed to have been erected by Hannibal. King Fernando III conquered the area in the 13th century and made it much larger. There are great views of the city from the Torre del Homenaje. Next to the castle is a mock-baronial *parador* hotel whose bar/restaurant is open to non-guests.

Open: summer Tue–Sun 10am–2pm & 5–9pm; winter Tue–Sun 10am–2pm & 3.30–7.30pm. Admission charge.

Catedral

The cathedral itself dwarfs the town almost as much as the castle – its twin towers are over 60m (197ft) high. Although the building was tinkered with by various architects over the centuries, including Andrés de Vandelvira, it's a masterpiece of Renaissance architecture. The cathedral museum holds some important religious artefacts from around the region.

Jaén's enormous cathedral looming above the old town

Catedral: Plaza de la Constitución/Santa María. Open: Mon–Sat 8.30am–1pm & 5–8pm, Sun 9am–1.30pm & 6–8pm (closed: Jul–Sept Sun pm).
Free admission.
Catedral Museum: open: Tue–Sat 10.30am–1pm & 5–8pm, Sun 10.30am–1pm & 6–8pm.
Admission charge.

Museo Provincial

This small museum dedicated to local history is also worth a visit for its fascinating collection of Iberian sculptures dating from around the 5th century BC and displaying a marked Greek influence, further suggesting an early Greek presence.

Paseo de la Estación. Open: Tue 2.30–8.30pm, Wed–Sat 9am–8.30pm, Sun 9am–2.30pm. Admission charge, free admission to EU citizens.

Parque Natural de Cazorla

The peaks, slopes and thickly wooded valleys of the Parque Natural de Cazorla, Segura y las Villas were once the preferred shooting fiefdom of Franco and his cronies. Now they have been gathered together as Spain's largest nature reserve, taking up almost a fifth of the area of Jaén province. There are still game hunters at large, but little disturbs the peace of this beautiful corner of Andalucía.

Cazorla

Clinging to the mountainside in the sierra of the same name, the town of Cazorla could almost be alpine with its jumble of gable-roofed houses and steep streets and alleys. It serves as an information office and service centre for the nature reserve, with a wide choice of accommodation and reasonably good transport links. It is a place of some history, having Roman remains and two Moorish castles, one in the town and one just outside it (**La Yedra**), which contains a folk museum. Another interesting monument is the ruined 16th-century church, the Iglesia de Santa María, which was razed by Napoleon's troops in the Peninsular War.

Several companies based in Cazorla offer guided walks and outdoor activities in the reserve, including the following:
Aventura Sport, Carretera de Huesa. Tel: 953 71 42 18.
www.aventurasport.com
Tierraventura Cazorla, Calle Ximénez de Rada 17. Tel: 953 71 00 73.
www.tierraventura.com

The road through the reserve

A single main road leads from Cazorla under the castle of La Iruela and over the **Puerto de las Palomas**, before descending to a crossroads, the Empalme del Valle. Most visitors turn northeast up the valley from here, but the *parador* (part of a chain of luxury, state-run hotels) makes an interesting visit, not because of the building itself, which is modern, but for its beautiful location. A long detour from the

Cazorla and its castles

crossroads (return trip of about 40km/ 25 miles) leads to the source of the Río Guadalquivir.

The road down the valley brings you instead to the **Torre del Vinagre Visitors' Centre**, which has a botanic garden next to it. There is also a hunting museum and, not far away, a fish farm. Deer and mouflon can be seen living in semi-liberty in the game park of **Parque Cinegético del Collado del Almendral**.

From the visitors' centre a scenic route runs beside an elongated reservoir, the Embalse del Tranco,

towards more open country at the north of the reserve. A left turn through the gorge of the upper Guadalquivir returns you to the olive-growing hills and plains of Jaén at Iznatoraf.

Segura de la Sierra

In the far north of the nature reserve is this town, which was important in Moorish times, as testified by its Arab baths and walls. Its magnificent castle – visible long before you get near the town – was built in the 13th and 14th centuries when Segura was ruled by the Knights of Santiago. There are impressive views from the top of the *torre del homenaje* (keep). The peak of **El Yelmo** at 1,805m (5,922ft) is popular among hang-gliders.

Nearby Hornos is another hill town dominated by a castle.

Úbeda and Baeza

Úbeda and Baeza are two Renaissance gems: old town centres composed of handsome palaces and churches, which were built between the 15th and 17th centuries when riches flowed into the region. None of the monuments here is of singular interest: it is the harmony of the whole which is so attractive – the pleasing streets and squares, and the details you come across. The historic centre of Úbeda is a UNESCO World Heritage Site. Both these towns are great places to stroll around at leisure.

Both Úbeda and Baeza trace their histories back to the Roman presence, but the towns we see today were created after the Reconquest, when both fell to the Christians within a short time of each other in the 13th century. Each was built by the newly landed gentry created by the *Reyes Católicos*, although this process was not without its tensions. Inter-clan rivalries in Úbeda grew so fierce that the royal family had the town walls demolished so that the army could intervene in the battles raging between its dynasties (after whom most of the streets are named).

Baeza

Baeza too had its awkward customers: Isabel ordered that its Alcázar be torn down because sparring families kept using it as a redoubt in their violent squabbles.

The Renaissance marvels that remain intact are a short stroll from the central Plaza de España and Paseo de la Constitución. Just off the southern tip of Plaza de España is Baeza's most striking Renaissance palace, the **Palacio de Jabalquinto**, and next to it the **Antigua Universidad** (Old University). Nearby is the town's cathedral, **Catedral de Santa María**, with a nave by Vandelvira.

Palacio de Jabalquinto: Calle Romanones (patio only). Open: Mon–Fri 9am–2pm. Free admission.

Catedral de Santa María: Plaza de Santa María. Open: daily Jun–Sept 10.30am–1pm & 5–7pm; Oct–May 10.30am–1pm & 4–6pm. Free admission.

Ayuntamiento Originally the town court and prison, this remarkable building dates from 1559; parts of it are open to the public. On the corner is the (private) house once occupied by Antigua Universidad employee, poet Antonio Machado. The greatest concentration of Renaissance palaces is north of here.

Ayuntamiento: Calle Benavides. Tel: 953 74 01 54. Open: by arrangement only.

(*Cont. on p134*)

Walk: Quesada and Tíscar

The mountain routes above Cazorla offer some spectacular views. This route, largely on roads, involves some improvisation with transport, or some serious hiking. There are numerous off-road routes around Cazorla, best taken with the guidance of one of the travel companies in the town, but they require at least a two-day stay in Cazorla.

This route can be completed in half a day, although you might want a taxi ride for part(s) of the route.

1 Quesada

Quesada is a small mountain village with little tourism, although it has an intriguing museum devoted to local painter Rafael Zabaleta.

2 Puerto de Tíscar

The road south towards Tíscar rises into the mountains below spectacular cliffs to the east (your left). Views in the opposite direction are out over the Sierra de Cazorla and the sea of olive groves

Olive groves between Cazorla and Quesada

below, and just get better and better. The little-used road (a particular favourite of locals) winds up through pines to the plateau of the Puerto de Tíscar, the Tíscar Pass. At 1,800m (5,905ft), this is only 200m (656ft) below the peak of Cabañas, the elephantine mountain looming over Cazorla. Views back, and, shortly, forwards, are stunning, perfected only if you climb up to the Moorish *atalaya* (watchtower), a short clamber up from the road.

3 Tíscar

From here the road begins to wind down towards the hamlet of Tíscar, below increasingly dramatic cliffs and overhangs, and, as often as not, raptors circling on thermals. As Tíscar comes into view below, so does a distinctly architectural shape in the jagged rock formations silhouetted above it. This is the Santuario de Tíscar, a Moorish fort built on a dizzying perch above the gorge carrying the Río Quesada. The fort was captured by the Christians in the early 14th century and turned into a shrine to the Virgin Mary. Today, it boasts a painting by Zabaleta recording Quesada's annual *romería* (religious procession) to the Virgin here.

There are a number of restaurants here, overlooking the river, where you might stop for lunch or arrange for a Cazorla taxi to collect you.

4 Huesa

A right-hand turning just beyond Tíscar leads down to Huesa and a lower route returning to Quesada.

5 Source of the Guadalquivir River

Alternatively, the same road on from Tíscar continues up on to the flank of Cabañas, past an extensive fire-damaged area of forest, and to a turning off which will lead, at some distance, to the source of the Guadalquivir, a journey only really viable by 4WD.

Instead of taking the Huesa turning, you can make a much longer walk by continuing in the direction of Pozo Alcón from Tíscar and taking the left turn under the peaks of Palomas and Cabañas to reach the Nacimiento del Río Guadalquivir. From here you can either go over Puerto Larente to Cazorla, or walk down the Guadalquivir valley to join the main road through the nature reserve beyond Puente de las Herrerias.

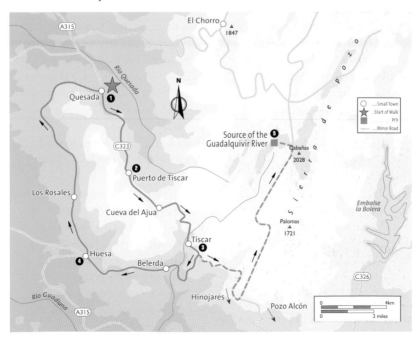

Úbeda's Plaza Vázquez de Molina

Úbeda

The old centre of Úbeda is so postcard-perfect it could be a film set. Between Plaza de Andalucía and the southerly town walls near Puerta de Granada, magnificent palaces and mansions jostle for attention along its cobbled streets and squares. At its heart sits the Plaza Vázquez de Molina, named after one of the aforementioned feuding families. This one square boasts no fewer than five buildings by Renaissance master Andrés de Vandelvira. On the west side is the **Palacio de las Cadenas**, which now houses the *ayuntamiento*. At its eastern end is the Gothic church of **Santa María de los Reales Alcázares**, the neighbouring **Cárcel del Obispo**, and

across from this the **Palacio de Marqués de Mancera**, which faces the **Palacio del Condestable Dávalos**, nowadays Úbeda's *parador*. There are more Vandelvira buildings to be found in the neighbouring Plaza del Primero de Mayo and nearby streets. The remaining city walls encircling the *casco antiguo* can be circumnavigated in under an hour.

There is only one important building not in the city centre – also by Vandelvira (in fact considered his best and most mature work): the **Hospital de Santiago** was built as a poor hospital, and now stands stranded in the outskirts near the bullring. It has a sombre but decorated façade, and a monumental staircase.

CÓRDOBA PROVINCE
Córdoba

Córdoba is one of the three great cities of Andalucía, along with Seville and Granada. Uniquely among European cities, it focuses on a mosque – one of immense historical and architectural significance – and it is this that most visitors come to see. But Córdoba's reputation rests on much more than that: it also has a castle, palaces, several good museums and above all a warren of medieval streets and leafy patios to explore.

Archaeologists have tracked agricultural settlements here back to the Neolithic period (4000–2000 BC) and have found evidence of trade – possibly seaborne, with olive-tree-bearing Greeks – dating back to the second millennium BC. Córdoba, or Corduba as it was named, became an important city under Roman rule in the 2nd century BC, and from 152 BC was the capital of Rome's Hispania Ulterior, the northernmost region of Baetica (Roman Spain) and roughly the size and shape of Andalucía. The city prospered on agriculture and mining, and produced the poets Lucan (AD 39–65) and Seneca (AD 4–65), tutor and ill-fated mentor to Nero.

With Roman influence in decline, Córdoba – like the rest of the Iberian peninsula – fell prey to Visigoth and Vandal insurgence. The city was taken by the Moors in 711, the same year that Tariq ibn Ziyad landed at Gibraltar. In 756 it was declared the capital of

Moorish Spain, under Abd ar-Rahman, who proclaimed himself the emir, independent ruler, of al-Andalus, and head of the Omayyad dynasty. Ar-Rahman oversaw the building of the Mezquita (mosque) between 785 and 787 – later rulers would expand and alter it (see pp136–7).

By 929, with Abd ar-Rahman III now self-declared caliph and wholly independent of Baghdad, Córdoba was the largest city in Europe. In effect, the concentration of knowledge, culture and power made Córdoba the centre of the Western world. This high-water mark in the city's history would produce such thinkers as Averroës and Maimónides (see p139).

The Omayyad dynasty was torn apart in the 11th century by internecine battles between rival Berber tribes and insurgent Christian *Reconquista* armies from the north. Córdoba slipped into the shadow of Seville, and finally fell to the Christians in 1236. It then entered a period of economic and political decline that was only reversed in the latter half of the 20th century.

Today, Córdoba is a compact and walkable city, with its *casco antiguo* centred, naturally, on the Mezquita, and the later, post-Reconquest, city built around and east of the central Plaza de las Tendillas. The city centre is shaped by the curving Río Guadalquivir as it passes the easterly limits of the old town.

While the Mezquita is a tourist honeytrap, perhaps unfortunately so given the level of vulgar commercialisation clustered around its walls, there is much more to Córdoba, as can be found on an easy stroll around the old town (*see pp138–9*).

Alcázar de los Reyes Cristianos

Alfonso XI had this fortress built in 1368, and it was used by Isabel and Fernando during their campaign to conquer Granada. It was later used by the Inquisition and, later still, as a prison, until the mid-20th century. The depredations of time have erased much of the earlier detail, but it retains beautiful mosaics and other artefacts in the interior, and landscaped gardens and waterways in the grounds.
Calle Caballerizas Reales.
Tel: 957 42 01 51. Open: mid-Sept–mid-Jun Tue–Fri 8.30am–7.30pm, Sat 9.30am–4.30pm, Sun 9.30am–2.30pm; mid-Jun–mid-Sept Tue–Sat 8.30am–2.30pm, Sun 9.30am–2.30pm. Admission charge; but free on Wed.

Medina Azahara

As well as declaring himself caliph, Abd ar-Rahman III also built an entirely new capital 7km (4 miles) west of the city. At its peak, Medina Azahara was an ambitious creation: one hall prefigured holographics by employing crystals to create man-made rainbows, while another used a vast pan of mercury tilted by a slave to produce lightning effects to impress the caliph's visitors. For 30 years until its perhaps inevitable destruction, ar-Rahman dedicated a

third of the caliphate's annual wealth to this bizarre indulgence, named after a favourite wife, az-Zahra. Abd ar-Rahman was eventually sidelined by one of his viziers, Ibn Abi Amir, later known as Al-Mansur (the victor), but Amir's attempts to construct his own caliphate were thwarted by civil war among various factions. Medina Azahara was razed by Berber mercenaries, and only rediscovered at the beginning of the 20th century. Barely a fraction of the site has been uncovered, but a series of vestigial structures can be seen while excavations continue.
Open: mid-Sept–Apr Tue–Sat 10am–6.30pm, Sun 10am–2pm; May–mid-Sept Tue–Sat 10am–8.30pm, Sun 10am–2pm. Admission charge; free to EU citizens.

La Mezquita

Córdoba's Mezquita (mosque) is unique in Europe: an (almost) intact 10th-century Moorish place of worship, and a stunning example of Moorish architecture. Parts were later destroyed (although some time after the Reconquest) to allow the construction of a Christian cathedral, but not even this act of desecration can reduce the effect of the artwork or the exquisite *mihrab* (prayer niche).

The Mezquita actually dates from a variety of eras, incorporating various architectural styles and materials from Visigothic and even Roman times. The building we see today was built in four distinct stages (five if we include the cathedral). The first stage, inwards from the Puerta de San Esteban and including the Patio de los Naranjos, was built in 785 by Abd ar-Rahman I on the site of a Visigothic church, although much of his original design disappeared under the 16th-century cathedral. As would be the case elsewhere in the mosque, his architect Sidi ben Ayub incorporated materials, including the exterior wall, from an earlier Visigothic cathedral that had stood on the site.

The Mezquita at Córdoba is probably the most exquisite Muslim monument in the West

Ayub's design was extended by Rahman I's successor Abd ar-Rahman II and again in the 10th century by Al-Hakam II, who added the grand, ornamented *mihrab*. The oblong shape seen today was completed in the last years of the 10th century by Al-Mansur. His chief contribution was to extend the prayer hall to something the size of a football pitch, with an arched roof requiring 850 columns of granite, jasper and marble. Again, a great deal of this material was taken from earlier structures, including Visigothic and Roman places of worship. As the mosque could not be extended further to the south because of the river, Al-Mansur extended it east. The Moorish arches, themselves an improvisation on an earlier Visigothic arch pattern, used alternating brick and stone to achieve the red and white motif, an innovation in Moorish architecture. At its finest, the mosque was the second largest in the world, and it is said that up to 40,000 people could pray in it at any one time.

Catedral The cathedral at the heart of the mosque wasn't in fact begun until 1523, after three centuries of minor tinkering with the original structure. The first Christian edifice to be built within the mosque was the Capilla de Villaviciosa, built by Moorish craftsmen in 1371, followed by the Mudéjar-style Puerta del Perdón. The most serious effect of this was to wall in the prayer (*Cont. on p140*)

Walk: Moorish Córdoba

The old town is a beautiful place for a stroll, especially during the Feria de los Patios in the first week of May, when the inhabitants of the older houses decorate their patios with plants, pots, mirrors and water features.

This short walk can be completed in under an hour. If you are visiting for the day by bus or train you can enter the old town via the Puerta de Almodóvar at the bottom of the Jardines de la Victoria and begin the walk there.

1 Torre de Calahorra

The walk begins across the river at the Torre de Calahorra. Although it was built after Córdoba fell to the Christians, nowadays the tower contains a small museum dedicated to Córdoba's Moorish history and a rather portentous homily on the family of man.
Tel: 957 29 39 29.
www.torrecalahorra.com. Open: daily Oct–Apr 10am–6pm; May–Sept 10am–2pm & 4.30–8.30pm. Admission charge.

2 Calle de Torrijos

Cross the Puente Romano (the Moorish waterwheel on your left is a

The Mezquita tower

reconstruction), pausing briefly by the Puerta del Puente gate to admire the city's patron saint, San Rafael, atop his 18th-century monument. Straight ahead is Calle de Torrijos, flanked on the right by the **Mezquita** (*see pp136–7*) and on the left by the **Palacio Episcopal** which houses a museum of sacred art. There is also a tourist information office near here.

Commercialisation is fairly intense in the streets immediately around the Mezquita, although at least you can find a drink or meal here. There are also shops and bars spread around the quieter areas away from the mosque.

3 Calle Blanco

Turn left by the Torre del Alminar, the site of the Mezquita's original minaret, on to Cardenal Herrero, where the modern *parador* is built on the site of a Moorish palace. At the end of Cardenal Herrero, walk round to Calle Blanco, which gives on to a number of *callejones* (alleys), including the famous Callejón de las Flores, whose walls and courtyards erupt with flowers in spring and especially during the Feria de los Patios.

4 Plaza Maimónides and the Judería

From Calle Blanco, retrace your steps via Calle Conde Y Luque to Calle Deanes, turn right on Calle Romero then left up to Plaza Maimónides, where a statue of the great Moorish philosopher marks the site of his home. Here also is the small **Museo Taurino** (Bullfighting Museum; closed for restoration), which celebrates, among others, Córdoban legend Manolete – not to mention Islero, the bull who gored Manolete to death during a *corrida* at Linares in 1947 and whose hide is displayed beside a replica of the matador's tomb. This is the heart of the Judería, the old Jewish quarter, and the site of the former **Sinagoga** (*tel: 957 20 29 28. Open: Tue–Sat 9.30am–2pm & 3.30–5pm, Sun 9.30am–1.30pm. Admission charge; free to EU citizens*), with some fascinating Hebrew texts fashioned in Mudéjar style. This is one of just three remaining synagogues left since the Jews were driven out of Spain after the Reconquest.

5 Puerta de Almodóvar

Just beyond the synagogue, Calle de Cairuan and Calle Puerta de Almodóvar will take you to the Puerta de Almodóvar, convenient if you're heading back to the train or bus station. Otherwise, Avenida Doctor Fleming leads down to Plaza Campo de los Martires, where there is a ruined Moorish *hammam* (bath) and the Alcázar. Beyond this is the river.

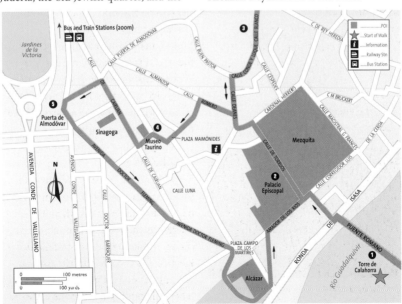

hall that had previously been open to the Patio de los Naranjos, where the faithful had prepared for prayer. What had been a light and airy place of worship became a dark and gloomy place of atonement.

Curiously, given the history of post-Reconquest Spain, the Córdoban authorities exercised considerable restraint in their handling of the building. It would seem that the religious authorities wanted to impose a Christian edifice on the Mezquita, and in 1523 King Carlos I overruled the advice of the Córdobans and authorised the project. Famously, Carlos regretted the result of his decision, telling the cathedral architects, 'You have destroyed something that was unique in the world.'

Monument to Maimónides in Córdoba

Calle Torrijos 10. Tel: 957 47 05 12. www.mezquitacatedral.es. Open: Mon–Sat 8.30am–6pm, Sun 8.30–10am & 2–6pm, although times can vary month by month; closes 5pm in winter. Admission charge.

Museo Arqueológico

As befits a city groaning with so much history, Córdoba's archaeological museum offers an excellent introduction to its prehistoric, Roman and Moorish past. The 16th-century mansion housing the museum, Casa Páez, contains an authentic Roman mosaic discovered during renovation work.

Plaza de Jerónimo Páez. Tel: 957 35 55 17. Open: Tue 2.30–8.30pm, Wed–Sat 9am–8.30pm, Sun 9am–2.30pm. Admission charge, free to EU citizens.

Museo de Bellas Artes and Palacio de Viana

While many of its paintings were siphoned off to the Prado, the Museum of Fine Arts still contains works by Murillo, Leal and Zurbarán. The Palacio de Viana is a museum dedicated to the Viana family, who began the palace in the 14th century and whose heirs sold it in the 1980s. The guided tour is perhaps not the most informative, but the palace has no fewer than a dozen superb patios.

Museo de Bellas Artes: Plaza del Potro. Tel: 957 35 55 48. Open: Tue 2.30–8.30pm, Wed–Sat 9am–8.30pm, Sun

A colourful courtyard in Córdoba

9am–2.30pm. Admission charge, free to EU citizens.
Palacio de Viana: Plaza de Gome. Tel: 957 49 67 41. Open: Tue–Fri 10am–7pm, Sat & Sun 10am–3pm. Last admission one hour before closing time. Admission charge.

Plazas

Córdoba's past and present meet in its squares. Plaza del Potro was once a livestock market and the area had a fairly rough reputation for centuries. Renovated, it is home to the **Posada del Potro**, named in *Don Quixote* and nowadays a contemporary art gallery. Plaza de las Tendillas is the centre of the modern city, but this is also the area where you will find many of Córdoba's historic churches (which are usually locked outside service hours and best visited around early evening).

Almodóvar del Río's impressive hilltop castle

Posada del Potro. Tel: 957 48 50 01. Open: Mon–Sat 5–9pm, although times can vary. Free admission.

Around Córdoba

Most visitors to Córdoba tend to concentrate their time in the capital – with, perhaps, a foray to Medina Azahara – and they leave with barely a glance at the province around it. Although this extends from vast, monotonous olive groves in the south to the desolate slopes of the Sierra Morena in the north, it includes some

sights worth the effort of getting to, including Spain's 'alternative' sherry centre, a handsome Baroque town and an enchanting mini-mountain range with its own white towns.

Almodóvar del Río

Although built originally by the Arabs in 760, this magnificent castle above a town on the Río Guadalquivir, 17km (11 miles) downstream from Córdoba, is largely a reconstruction. It plays on a faux historical theme offering visitors all things medieval:

a gift shop, banquets, markets and a programme of cultural events on the same theme.
www.castillodealmodovar.com.
Open: Mon–Fri 11am–2.30pm &
4–7pm, Sat & Sun 11am–7pm
(closes 8pm in summer).
Admission charge.

Montilla

Jerez de la Frontera (*see pp63–5*) may get all the fame with its sherry, but Córdoba's equivalent town of Montilla claims its wines are just as good without any need to fortify them. Still, at least it gets remembered in the name Amontillado – the term for pale, dry sherry. Several of the wine producers (*bodegas*) will give you a tour. The largest is Alvear, which also claims to be the oldest *bodega* in Spain.

At the opposite end of town from **Bodegas Alvear** are the Mudéjar-style convent of Santa Clara with a carved portal, and the Casa del Inca, the former home of Garcilaso de la Vega, Spain's historian of the Incas.

Aguilar de la Frontera, a short way south of Montilla, has a grand 19th-century octagonal main square. **Fernán Núñez**, to the north, on the way to Córdoba city, is dominated by the palace of the Dukes of Fernán Núñez, built in the 1780s, with a restored formal terraced garden behind it.
Bodegas Alvear: Avenida María Auxiliadora. Tel: 957 65 29 39.
www.alvear.eu. Open: visits Mon–Fri 12.30pm, Sat & Sun by appointment
only (minimum seven people). Reserve your visit in advance if possible.
Admission charge.

Priego de Córdoba

Córdoba province's finest town was filled with Baroque architecture during the 17th and 18th centuries on the proceeds of the silk and textile industry. The chief sight is a fountain, La Fuente del Rey, consisting of three ornamental basins fed by 139 spouts. Priego also has a pretty Moorish quarter to explore, the Barrio de la Villa.

Sierra Subbética

It may not be as famous or as much visited as some of Andalucía's other mountain ranges, but the Sierra Subbética has its share of attractive scenery and interesting villages. The best place to stay overnight is **Zuheros**, a cluster of winding streets of brilliant white houses beneath a castle. Above the town is the **Cueva de los Murciélagos**, a 2km (1¼-mile) -long cave decorated with Stone Age paintings, of which 450m (1,476ft) with 700 steps is open to the public.

Two towns on the edge of the sierra worth visiting are **Baena**, famed for its high-quality olive oil, and **Cabra**, which has several old churches and aristocratic mansions.
Cueva de los Murciélagos: Tel: 957 69 45 45. www.cuevadelosmurcielagos.com.
Open: Mon–Fri 12.30–5.30pm (closes 4.30pm in winter). Sat & Sun by appointment only. Admission charge.

Bike Tour: Sierra Subbética Green Way

The route of the Tren del Aceite (Olive Oil Train) through the hills of the Sierra Subbética, south of Córdoba, is now a surfaced cycle track. It's well marked so you can't get lost. Plus there are no steep gradients – although you'll need to climb hills to visit the prettiest villages. In summer, it's best to avoid pedalling in the middle of the day. Always take water, sunblock and a hat.

The cycle track is 58km (39 miles) long and can be completed in a day by a fit person but is better split into two days.

1 Reserva Natural de la Laguna del Salobral

The line starts at a bridge over the Guadajoz River and passes near this wetland nature reserve which is home to ducks and waders. It is at its most interesting in spring and early summer when it is fringed with wild flowers.

2 Luque

The first main stop is Luque where there is a restaurant using some of the line's old rolling stock.

3 Zuheros

A short detour uphill is one of the most attractive towns in the province of Córdoba, a compact huddle of houses

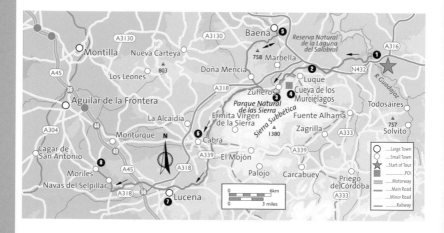

The pretty rooftops of Zuheros

beneath a small castle. Hotel Zuhayra (*Calle Mirador 10. Tel: 957 69 46 93*) has bicycles available for the use of its guests

4 Cueva de los Murciélagos

Before you go downhill from Zuheros, you might want to visit the 'Cave of the Bats', which has prehistoric pictures on its walls dating from approximately 18,000 BC. *See also p143.*

5 Baena

If you have the stamina, you may want to make an excursion 7km (4 miles) north to Baena which produces some of the best olive oil in Spain. It has a Moorish castle, 16th-century convent and a church with an Isabelline portal.

6 Cabra

Heading west from Zuheros takes you via Doña Mencía to Cabra where the town station has been turned into an information centre, the Centro de Interpretación del Tren del Aceite. It includes a cafeteria and a small museum.

7 Lucena

Lucena also has an information centre in its old station doubling as a museum of arts and traditions of the town.

8 Moriles

The green way comes to an end in vineyard country. Moriles, a few kilometres to the north, makes fortified wines which the locals consider superior to sherry.

The main drawback to green ways is that they are linear and the fastest and most scenic way back to your starting point is the way you came. A longer, scenic alternative is via Priego de Córdoba using the A339 and A333.

The Reconquest

The term 'Reconquest' is a misnomer, but so in this context are the words 'Spain' and 'Moor'. Prior to Tariq ibn Ziyad's invasion of AD 711, there was no unified 'Spain' to be reconquered, rather a ragbag of small kingdoms jockeying for power, at odds with their neighbours and often found in cahoots with parts of what would later become France, Holland or Germany. Similarly, 'Moor' is a particularly wide brush used to paint numerous North African cultures.

The Reconquest was an ideological battle, as the gusto with which Isabel and Fernando pursued their agenda suggests. Having ejected the barbarians, the *Reyes Católicos* set about expelling Protestants, Jews, Morisco 'converts' and anyone else who disagreed with them. In modern terms, the Reconquest might be seen more as the ethnic cleansing of various peoples who had lived in Andalucía for centuries. It was also a battle to reassert vested interests: a tiny aristocratic elite became immensely wealthy by appropriating al-Andalus from the Moors.

This noted, we should also reconsider the 'Moors'. Recent decades have seen historians turning against the 'Eurocentric' reading of the Reconquest that sided with the armies of God against the armies of Mohammed. As any visitor to Seville, Granada or Córdoba will see, the Moors brought great learning to al-Andalus. A journey through modern Andalucía will also show what their water technologies did to the near deserts here. Yet the successive waves of North African invaders were just as bellicose as their opponents, and capable of equal cruelty. The fact that it took one 'side' 709 years to win and the other 709 years to lose is surely a measure of the ferocity of the armies on both sides.

The element of surprise

The real surprise was the ease with which the Berbers took the southwesternmost tip of Spain, sweeping north and meeting their first real resistance at Jerez in AD 712, where they defeated King Rodrigo and his army and effectively took control of Spain.

The Reconquest is commonly taken to have begun in AD 722 with the semi-legendary Christian victory at Covadonga in Asturias, one of the few regions not to have been overrun by the Moors. For the next few hundred years or so, battlelines rippled back and forth across the Iberian landscape, frequently depositing the suffix 'de la Frontera' (of the frontier) on spots on the map where the Christians established a foothold. The turning point came, finally, with the Christian victory at Las Navas de Tolosa, in northern Jaén, in 1212. Yet it would be another 280 years before the final Moorish stronghold, Granada, fell.

It used to be said that there were houses in Cairo, Tangier and elsewhere where the keys to houses in Granada, Ronda and other Andalucian cities still hung over the mantelpiece until such time as their rightful owners could reclaim them from the infidels. The Moors, of course, never really went away. They are still here in the gene pool, in the architecture and in the name.

Waterwheels used to irrigate the Alcázar gardens at Córdoba

Getting away from it all

From the deserted beaches of the Costa de la Luz to the ski slopes of the Sierra Nevada, and from the dune systems of Almería to the primordial forests of the Sierra de Grazalema, Andalucía boasts a variety of landscapes unrivalled in the rest of Spain. With a car or timetables for trains and buses, almost all of them are within easy reach of even the largest cities.

Exploring the Andalucian countryside

Andalucía has two national parks (Doñana and the Sierra Nevada) and twenty more large nature reserves, all of which means there are plenty of good places to go walking. Popular areas include the Alpujarras, the Sierra de Grazalema and Cazorla.

If you want a serious hike you could try following one of the region's nine long-distance footpaths (GR). Most challenging in length is the GR7 'Mediterranean Arc' which links the Aegean and the Atlantic. There are plenty of much shorter marked walking routes classified as PR–A and graded from *baja* (easy) to *muy alta* (extremely demanding).

However experienced you are, there are some common-sense precautions to take. The weather is usually better in spring and early summer – and there are lots of wild flowers to see. The heat can build up in the summer months, and if you want to go walking in either

July or August do so in the early morning or in the evening.

Stick to marked routes as much as possible and carry a map. Never go off into remote countryside alone and always tell someone where you will be. Wear a hat and make sure you have plenty of drinking water in your rucksack.

Reliable walking maps may not be on sale in the area where you are going and it is sensible to buy them beforehand. The Centro Nacional de Información Geográfica (CNIG, *www.cnig.es*) publishes a 1:25 000 series, and the Spanish army (Servicio Geográfico del Ejército) produces sheets to a scale of 1:50 000.

The best map shop is **Librería Índice** in Málaga (*Calle Panaderos 2. Tel: 900 15 05 40*).

For more information about walking in Andalucía, contact the **Federación Andaluza de Montañismo** (*Camino de Ronda 101, Granada. Tel: 958 29 13 40. www.fedamon.com*).

Portugal

From Huelva province it is only a short hop by motorway over the border into the Algarve region of southern Portugal. Within range of a day trip are the city of Faro, the lagoons and marshes of the Ria Formosa nature reserve and the pretty town and island of Tavira.

Morocco

Most of the coast between Málaga and Tarifa, and inland as far as Gaucín, has views of Africa floating on its southern horizon. Algeciras, Gibraltar and Tarifa have the quickest connections to ports such as Tangier, with over 20 different ferry and catamaran services a day: most Costa del Sol resorts and towns in western Andalucía will have agencies offering day trips and longer stopovers.

Both Málaga and Almería have ferries to the Spanish enclave of Melilla, while Ceuta can be reached from Algeciras. However, at six and seven hours one way, these are more extended trips and neither has the attractions of Tangier.

The largest operator of services to North Africa is Acciona Trasmediterránea (*Tel: 902 45 46 45. www.trasmediterranea.es*), with regular services from Algeciras to Tangier and Almería to Nador and Ghazaouet.

Morocco is a short ferry ride away

Shopping

Thanks to rising living standards and Spain's entry into the eurozone, Andalucía is no longer quite as cheap as it once was, but it is still a great place to shop. Avoid the brand stores and hypermarkets, and you'll find some real bargains in smaller shops and on market stalls.

Shoes, clothes, CDs, most foods, alcohol and cigarettes remain cheaper in Spain than in northern Europe. Books, stereos, computers and kitchen equipment are more expensive. IVA (VAT) is applied at two rates, 16 or 7 per cent, depending on the goods or services in question. Most tourist shops usually offer tax-free shopping for non-EU citizens.

Seville, Granada and Marbella, and to a lesser extent Cádiz, Córdoba, Jaén, Jerez and Málaga, have shopping districts to match any northern European city.

WHERE TO BUY
El Corte Inglés

Spain's home-grown department store is a good one-stop shop for almost everything you need including clothes, electrical goods, toiletries, books, magazines and newspapers in English, and maps. There is usually a supermarket, too, which stocks gourmet and imported international foods. The emphasis is on quality rather than rock-bottom prices; it may not be the cheapest place in town but there again it is rarely the most expensive. There are branches of El Corte Inglés in Seville (five), Cádiz, Algeciras, Córdoba, Granada, Huelva, Jaén, Jerez de la Frontera, Linares, Málaga and Marbella.
www.elcorteingles.es

Street markets

Most villages and towns have a weekly street market with a variety of stalls selling mainly fresh food and functional household items but also clothes, shoes and crafts.

WHAT TO BUY
Books

Lavish production values make Spanish books objects of desire, although foreign-language editions are rare. University cities such as Seville have at least one shop with a foreign-language section. English books are available at:

Librería Vértice

San Fernando 33 (opposite the university), Seville. Tel: 954 21 16 54. www.libreriavertice.com

Nerja Book Centre

Second-hand books.

Calle Granada 30–32, Nerja. Tel: 952 52 09 08. www.nerjatoday.com

Clothing

It takes immense cool to carry off wearing Spanish men's hats and even more so the *mantilla* and *peineta* (shawl and ornamental comb), but if you can they're worth the expense. *Gitana* dresses and *trajes de luces* are other popular souvenirs.

Bordados Foronda

Calle Sierpes 33, Seville. Tel: 954 22 76 61. www.juanforonda.com

Hoss Intropia

Modern women's designer clothing.

O'Donnell 16, Seville. Tel: 954 50 26 75. www.hossintropia.com

Pedro Algaba

A bullfighter's suit (*traje de luces*) would be an expensive souvenir, but in this shop next to the Maestranza bullring there are cheaper items on sale including capes, hats, posters and other bullfighting gear.

Adriano 39, Seville. Tel: 954 27 78 72.

Crafts

The cities and countryside are excellent hunting grounds for crafts, both indigenous and imported. Andalucía produces numerous forms of glazed and matt pottery such as Granada's distinctive blue-and-green design of Fajalauza pottery, and the Lucena pottery in Córdoba, with geometric green-and-yellow design that can be seen in its traditional *botijos* (drinking pitchers). Traditional fans and *mantillas* (embroidered shawls) and the superb handcrafted Spanish guitars also make excellent souvenirs. There is embossed

A Seville street stall

leather, marquetry and metal craftwork with traditional Islamic patterns. Córdoba is particularly noted for silver filigree jewellery, and there are outlets throughout town – Zoco Municipal (*Calle Judíos*) is a pretty courtyard where you can watch craftspeople at work in their workshops. In Granada, there are Moroccan handicraft and pottery shops around the Albaicín. Colourful rugs, cushions and bedspreads are available in the Alpujarras villages.

Ceramics

Albayalde Handmade Moorish tiles. *Cortijo del Cura, Órgiva, Alpujarras. Tel: 958 78 51 99.*
Cerámica Santa Ana Famous tile factory making elaborate mural ceramics, fountains and altarpieces. *San Jorge 31, Seville. Tel: 954 33 39 90.*

Guitars

Handmade guitars can be bought from the workshops on the Cuesta de Gomérez, on the way up to the Alhambra, in Granada.
José L Postigo Handcrafted Spanish guitars. *Hernando Colón 34, Seville. Tel: 954 21 38 15. www.guitarraspostigo.com*
Valeriano Bernal Handmade Spanish and flamenco guitars. *Hernando del Pulgar 20, Seville. Tel: 954 582 679. www.antoniobernal.com*

Leather goods

Spanish leather is famous for its quality and craftsmanship.

Meryan Workshop and shop. *Calleja de las Flores 2, Córdoba. Tel: 957 47 59 02. www.meryancor.com*

Woodwork

Laguna Taracea Traditional marquetry. *Calle Real de la Alhambra, Granada. Tel: 958 22 90 19. www.laguna-taracea.com*

Food

Certain foodstuffs, such as olive oils and cured meats, are uniquely Spanish and even uniquely Andalucian. Jaén is said to be the largest olive-growing region on the planet, and country lanes are full of signs offering virgin oil (*aceite virgen de oliva*) for sale. Similarly, the Atlantic Costa de la Luz is famed for its tuna, sardines and other fish, which can be found on delicatessen counters.

The range of fresh and preserved foodstuffs is vast and varies enormously across Andalucía. Spain's commendable resistance to processing and factory production ensures that its food is among the finest in Europe. As well as its forest regions' superb (if costly) olive and oak wood products, cured mountain hams are available in Trevélez and other villages in the Alpujarras.

Turronarte
Virgin olive oil, *turrón* (nougat) and local wines are on sale in this gourmet delicatessen. *Medina y Corella 2, Córdoba. Tel: 957 47 72 79.*

Local wickerwork for sale

Al Sur de Granada
Delicatessen stocking a fine range of hams from Trevélez in the Alpujarras and other produce from Granada province.
Calle Elvira 150, Granada.
Tel: 958 27 02 45.
www.alsurdegranada.net

Music and DVDs
New and bestselling CDs, DVDs and videos sell at similar prices to those in northern Europe, but, if you are willing to take pot luck, there are bargains to be had in discount stores where you will find a good choice of locally produced music.

Flamenco music
Compás Sur Excellent choice of flamenco music. *Cuesta del Rosario 7-F, Seville. Tel: 954 21 56 62.*
www.compas-sur.com

Wines
La Casa de Jerez
A good place to taste wines before you decide what to buy.
Divina Pastora 1, Jerez de la Frontera.
Tel: 956 33 51 84.
Tierra Nuestra
Local wines and from all over Spain. Also a wine club.
Cristóbal Sánchez Fuentes 1, Seville.
Tel: 954 27 62 72. www.tierranuestra.es

Entertainment

Andalucía offers a generous choice of entertainment from low- to high-brow, depending on your taste. Given the climate, the best things happen outside and it's common to see music, dance and theatre on open-air stages in public places. There are even open-air 'summer' cinemas where you can watch the latest Hollywood film in the cool of the night under the stars.

The Andalucian thirst for culture can be seen in the growing number of arts festivals, galleries and venues, and the pages of journalism dedicated to these at national, regional and local levels.

Agencies specialising in booking tickets for all entertainments include **Entradas** (*Tel: 902 22 16 22. www.entradas.com*) and **Servi Caixa** (*www.servicaixa.com*).

MUSIC
Flamenco

Many visitors to Andalucía hope to get a taste of authentic flamenco music and dance (*see pp18–19*). The discussion about what is and isn't authentic flamenco could go on forever. A die-hard flamenco expert would say that if a foreign tourist is watching it, it isn't the real thing; that the *duende* only appears spontaneously, behind closed doors, among gypsies and their friends. But it could easily be argued that flamenco is in constant evolution, has hybridised in a thousand equally valid ways and that,

when it is reduced to its essentials, it is a form of entertainment. In short, be discerning when choosing a show to see, avoiding those that obviously receive tour parties, and you'll see something close to the real thing. Lists of venues are available from local tourist information offices. Prices are generally not cheap, but often a drink or dinner is included.

Córdoba
Tablao El Cardenal Shows Mon–Sat at 10.30pm. *Calle Torrijos 10. Tel: 957 48 31 12. www.tablaocardenal.com*

Granada
Sala Albayzín Walking tour of the Albaicín and Sacromonte, and an introduction to flamenco before the show. *Carretera de Murcia, Mirador de San Cristóbal. Tel: 958 80 46 46. www.flamencoalbayzin.com*

Jerez de la Frontera
Jerez claims to be the joint birthplace of authentic flamenco (with Seville's

Triana) and for this reason it is home to the Centro Andaluz de Flamenco (*see pp63–4*). A good place to see and hear flamenco is:

La Taberna Flamenca Restaurant with flamenco show after lunch at 2.30pm (but check times before booking). *Angostillo de Santiago 3 (opposite the Iglesia de Santiago). Tel: 956 32 36 93. www.latabernaflamenca.com*

Seville

Triana claims to be the home of flamenco and there are several bars there giving impromptu or unadvertised shows. The better-known flamenco venues, however, are all in Santa Cruz. They include the new Museo del Baile Flamenco (*see p36*) and the following:

La Carbonería A bar in what were once a coal merchant's premises that has long had a reputation for the quality of its performances. *Levies 18. Tel: 954 21 44 60.*

Casa de la Memoria de Al Andalus A cultural centre dedicated to Andalucian traditional culture in general but especially flamenco, with shows nightly at 9pm. *Calle Ximénez de Enciso 28. Tel: 954 56 06 70. www.casadelamemoria.es*

Other music
Granada

The **Teatro Municipal Isabel La Católica** (*Acera del Casino. Tel: 958 22 15 14*), the **Teatro Alhambra** (*Calle Molinos 56. Tel: 958 02 80 00. www.teatroalhambra.com*) and the

Auditorio de Manuel de Falla (*Paseo de los Martíres. Tel: 958 22 29 07. www.manueldefalla.org*) serve the same function. The monthly free sheet *Guía de Granada* lists all performances.

There are also regular concerts in Almería, Cádiz, Córdoba and Málaga, as well as in smaller towns such as Ronda and Jerez, which are listed in the Andalucía-wide free monthly *¿Qué Hacer?* (What's On?), available in tourist offices and many hotels. Information about events in Andalucía is posted on the net at *www.Andalucia.org*

Seville

The **Teatro de la Maestranza** (*Paseo de Colón 22. Tel: 954 22 33 44. www.teatromaestranza.com*), **Teatro Lope de Vega** (*Avenida de María Luisa. Tel: 955 47 28 28. www.teatrolopedevega.org*) and **Teatro Central** on Isla de la Cartuja (*José de Gálvez. Tel: 955 03 72 00. www.teatrocentral.com*) are key venues for classical, jazz and pop music. Events are publicised around the city and in the monthly free sheet *El Giraldillo* (*www.elgiraldillo.es*), a listings magazine given away across the city.

THEATRE

The following theatres serve as chief venues for theatre and other events in towns noted for independent and touring productions.

A sign for a flamenco-dancing venue in Seville

Cádiz
Gran Teatro Falla
Plaza de Falla. Tel: 956 22 08 94.

Córdoba
Gran Teatro de Córdoba
Avenida Gran Capitán 3.
Tel: 957 48 02 37.
www.teatrocordoba.com

Jaén
Auditorio Municipal de la Alameda
Alameda de Calvo Sotelo.
Tel: 953 21 91 16. www.aytojaen.es
Teatro Darymelia
Calle de la Maestra 18. Tel: 953 21 91 80.

Málaga
Teatro Cánovas
Plaza el Ejido 5. Tel: 951 30 89 02.
www.teatrocanovas.es
Teatro Cervantes
Calle Ramos Marín. Tel: 952 22 41 00.
www.teatrocervantes.com

Nerja
Nerja Caves
One of the most remarkable venues is the Nerja Cave system, which holds ballet, music and theatre performances during summer months.
Tel: 952 52 95 20. www.cuevadenerja.es

CINEMA
Foreign-language films with subtitles are a rarity in Spain; most films are dubbed into Spanish. In university cities, however, and where there are concentrations of expat citizens on the Costa del Sol, it is increasingly common to see films advertised as VO – *versión original*. The norm, however, is the urban multi-screen cinema showing blockbuster US releases, peppered with Spanish and Latin American productions. On the coasts in summer there is another option – the *cine de verano*, a laid-back cinema open to the night sky. Even if you don't understand the action on screen it can be an enjoyable way to pass a couple of hours.

Córdoba
Filmoteca de Andalucía
Medina y Corella 5. Tel: 957 35 56 55.
www.filmotecadeandalucía.com

Granada
Centro de Lenguas Modernas (University of Granada)
Placeta del Hospicio Viejo.
Tel: 958 21 56 60.
www.clm-granada.com
Cine Club Universitario
Hospital Real, Cuesta del Hospicio.
Tel: 958 24 30 14. http://veucd.ugr.es

Marbella
Complejo Cinematográfico Gran Marbella
Between Hipercor and Puerto Banús.
Tel: 952 81 64 21.
www.cinesgranmarbella.com

Seville
Cineciudad
Marqués de Paradas 15.
Tel: 954 29 30 25. www.cineciudad.com

BARS, CLUBS AND DISCOTHEQUES

Andalucians go out late – after midnight is not unusual – particularly at the weekends and even more so in summer when the temperature is more comfortable at night. Hence many bars stay open way beyond the small hours even to daybreak. Most discotheques are in the outskirts and provide a free bus service so that partygoers are not tempted to drink and drive.

Seville

AB

An elegant nightclub for the over 30s, popular with footballers and local celebrities. *Avenida de la Buhaira 5. Tel: 954 58 40 89.*

Ateneo Café

An English-pub-style bar in Triana with a piano and a good cocktail list. *Avenida José María Martínez Sánchez-Arjona 23. Tel: 954 28 12 10.*

Bilindo

A summer outdoor discotheque located in the fantastic Parque de María Luisa. *Paseo de las Delicias, Plaza de América. Tel: 954 62 61 51. www.terrazabilindo.com*

Cádiz and Costa de la Luz
Cádiz

Arena Listen to jazz and bossa nova while enjoying the magnificent sea views from the terrace. *Avenida Amilcar Barca 17, Puerta de Tierra. Tel: 956 26 40 10.*

Café Teatro Pay Pay This popular café stages cabaret, concerts, exhibitions and also conferences. *Calle Silencio, Barrio del Populo. Tel: 956 25 25 43. www.cafeteatropaypay.com*

Huelva

Alameda This discotheque holds two sessions, one for young people and the second for the not so young. *Alameda Sundheim, Isla Chica. Tel: 959 26 13 06.*

Western Costa del Sol
Antequera

A la fuerza Opened as a cafeteria in 1917 and now a venerable restaurant and live music venue which also stages exhibitions. *Alhameda de Andalucía 32. Tel: 952 84 16 07. www.alafuerza.net*

Benalmádena

Disco Kiu A large discotheque with four different spaces creating four different atmospheres: modern, Spanish, Latin and eclectic. *Plaza de Solymar. Tel: 952 44 05 18. www.discotecakiu.com*

Fuengirola

Bogart Café You can dine and dance until 6am in this popular café. *Paseo Marítimo Rey de España, Complejo Las Palmeras. Tel: 952 47 00 91.*

Málaga

Aguanta This bar has a range of table games to play while sipping your drink. It also offers Internet connection.

Camino de la Termica 4.
www.baraguanta.com
El Pimpi A very popular *bodega* (traditional bar) in a renovated old convent. *Calle Granada 62.*
Tel: 952 22 89 90.

Marbella
Dreamer's International DJs are regularly invited to this famous discotheque. *Carretera de Cádiz, Km 175, Río Verde, facing Puerto Banús.*
Tel: 952 81 20 80.
www.dreamers-disco.com

Eastern Costa del Sol
Nerja
Theba's This bar, pub and disco plays mainly Spanish and Latin music with lots of rhythm. *Plaza Tutti Frutti, Local 3. Tel: 952 52 47 74.*
www.thebasnerja.com

Granada and Sierra de Nevada
Granada
Afrodisia Club Black music with reggae on Wednesdays and funk on Thursdays. *Almona del Boquerón, Edificio Corona.*
www.afrodisiaclub.com

A flamenco venue in Marbella

Bohemia Jazz Café Jazz lovers flock to this relaxed bar decorated in an early 20th-century style which, as well as alcoholic drinks, also serves milkshakes and hot chocolate. *Santa Teresa 17.*
Tel: 958 26 02 84.
www.bohemiajazzcafe.blogspot.com
Enano Rojo A very popular bar which stages live concerts. *Calle Elvira 91.*
Tel: 958 20 30 80.
www.myspace.com/barenanorojo
Granada 10 This city centre cinema in the afternoons becomes a very popular disco at night featuring disco, hip hop, Latin, salsa and merengue.
Cárcel Baja 10. Tel: 958 22 40 01.
www.granada10.com

Northern Andalucía
Córdoba
Al Baile You can dance here and also take ballroom dancing lessons. *Recinto Ferial El Arenal.*
Tel: 957 75 90 00. www.albaile.com
Café Málaga This bar features mainly jazz but also puts on *café-teatro* (cabaret). *Calle Málaga 3.*
Tel: 957 47 62 98.

Jaén
Abaco There's good music in this discotheque which is decorated in a very modern style. *Avenida Muñoz Grandes 4. Tel: 953 27 68 71.*
Atrium This discotheque is decorated in imitation of the Sistine Chapel. *Paseo de la Estación 33.*
Tel: 953 25 31 56.

Children

Anyone travelling with children in Andalucía will meet a particularly warm welcome almost everywhere. Children are integrated into Spanish social life to the extent that they can often be seen out with their parents until the small hours. Children will also have fun at the various fiestas throughout the province.

There's no shortage of activities for children on the Costa del Sol, and most parts of the coast and the major cities are within reach of a water park. The mosque at Córdoba and the Alhambra offer the challenge of finding your way around, and castles and caves can also be fun to explore. Many fiestas include spectacles especially for children, but all of them can be entertaining.

Doñana National Park

Older children who like wildlife and animals will enjoy a nature walk, 4WD excursion or boat ride in Spain's sensational nature reserve. *See pp62–3.*

Gibraltar

For its cable car and monkeys. *See pp89 & 92.*

Isla Mágica

Andalucía's premier theme park with white-knuckle and gentler rides, themed areas and shows. *See p43.*

Mini-Hollywood

The oldest of various Wild West theme attractions in the Tabernas area of Almería, and the place where they shot parts of *The Magnificent Seven, A Fistful of Dollars, The Good, the Bad and the Ugly* and dozens of other spaghetti Westerns. There are Wild West extravaganzas, cancan shows and a small zoo with events throughout the day. *See pp104–5.*

Parque de las Ciencias, Granada

Hands-on science park on the city outskirts, with planetarium, science games and various exhibitions pitched at bloodthirsty pre-teens. The planetarium also has viewings at its observatory, depending on sky conditions and season.
Avenida del Mediterráneo.
Tel: 958 13 19 00.
www.parqueciencias.com.
Open: Tue–Sat 10am–7pm, Sun 10am–3pm. Admission charge (separate charge for planetarium).

La Rábida

The key Columbus site is now a museum with historical displays and, at the *muelle* (jetty), there are life-sized models of his ships to explore. *See pp56–7.*

Real Escuela Andaluza de Arte Ecuestre

See pp64–5.

SELWO Aventura

Andalucía's largest wildlife park, with tours and aerial walkways through outdoor areas where animals dwell in habitats resembling 'natural' conditions. *Off A7 motorway Las Lomas Del Monte/Estepona. Tel: 902 19 04 82. www.selwo.es. Open: 10am–6pm (until 8pm in summer). Admission charge. Group and other discounts available, including Selwopack joint admission to Marina and Teleférico (see below).*

SELWO Marina

Aquarium attraction with dolphins, sea lions and penguins. *Parque de la Paloma, Benalmádena. Tel: 902 19 04 82. www.selwomarina.es. Open: 10am–6pm (later in summer). Admission charge.*

Teleférico Benalmádena

Panoramic cable-car rides into the hills above Torremolinos, where there are viewpoints and marked walks. *Esplanada Tivoli, Benalmádena. Tel: 902 19 04 82. www.telefericobenalmadena.com.*

Open: Jul & Aug 11am–3pm & 6pm–midnight; Sept–mid-Jan & mid-Feb–Jun 11am–7pm; closes at 5pm in winter. Admission charge. Does not run in bad weather – call for confirmation.

Tivoli World

The largest theme park on the Costa del Sol, with white-knuckle and gentler rides, gardens and shows. *Avenida de Tivoli, Arroyo de la Miel, Benalmádena. Tel: 952 57 70 16. www.tivoli.es. Open: Jul 5pm–1am, Aug 6pm–2am; opening times vary greatly throughout the rest of the year. Closed Dec. Admission charge (children under 1m (3ft 3ins) free admission).*

Children will enjoy the fiestas

Sport and leisure

Why laze on the beach doing nothing when you have the perfect climate for outdoor activities? Andalucía offers an extraordinary range of things to do. Watersports are an obvious attraction and the Costa del Sol is famed for its golf courses. Surprisingly, perhaps, one of Spain's largest ski resorts is only an hour from the south coast.

OUTDOOR PURSUITS

Andalucía's remoter regions all offer a variety of outdoor activities, such as hiking, horse riding, mountain biking, canoeing, caving, climbing, canyoning, parascending (*parapente*), hang-gliding and even ballooning. A number of companies also offer cuisine or dance classes. Below is a selection of some of these.

Astronomy
Hotel Salitre and Observatorio Astronómico
Hotel-campsite in the Serranía de Ronda with its own observatory and 9cm (3½in) reflector telescope.
Algatocín, Málaga. Tel: 952 11 70 05. www.turismosalitre.com

Ballooning
Glovento Sur
Balloon flights in the Granada region (Granada city, Guadix, Sierra Nevada, Antequera and elsewhere).
Tel: 958 29 03 16. www.gloventosur.com

Golf

The Costa del Sol has many of the region's best golf courses. The Federación Andaluza de Golf has more than 50 courses in Andalucía. Its website has information in Spanish and English.
Federación Andaluza de Golf
tel: 952 22 55 90. www.fga.org

Horse riding
Andalucian Horse-Riding Adventure
Half- or full-day rides in the mountains of the Sierra de las Nieves nature reserve. Overnight rides available.
Monda (inland from Marbella).
Tel: 952 11 23 63.
www.horseridingmarbella.com
Dallas Love
Horse-riding expeditions around Bubión in the Alpujarras and the Sierra Nevada.
Tel: 958 76 30 38.
www.spain-horse-riding.com
Los Alamos
Riding holidays around Cádiz natural parks and beaches.

Barbate, on the coast of Cádiz.
Tel: 956 43 10 47.
www.losalamosriding.co.uk

Nautical
El Cabo a Fondo
Expeditions by semi-rigid inflatables to parts of the spectacular Cabo de Gata peninsula, inaccessible by land.
Cabo de Gata. Tel: 637 44 91 70.
www.elcaboafondo.es

Skiing
For three to four months each winter the Sierra Nevada northeast of Granada becomes Europe's most southerly ski resort (*see p123*). Only half an hour by bus from Granada, the (rather modest) resort has over 50 slopes from nursery to black runs, skiboard runs, toboggan and sledging routes, as well as accommodation ranging from youth hostels to four-star hotels. The resort has online reservations and an interactive phone line offering weather reports and reservations.

Skydiving
Skydivespain
Accompanied 'tandem' parachute jumps, solo parachute jump courses (for groups), full, 'accelerated free fall' courses for skydiver qualification, and powered parachute flights.
Tel: 687 726 303. www.skydivespain.com

Specialist tours
For tours and activities in Cazorla nature reserve, see pp129–31.

Monte Aventura
Specialist in 4WD safaris and activity pursuits in the Sierra de las Nieves.
Tel: 952 88 15 19.
www.monteaventura.com

Walking
Andalucian Adventures
Walking holidays across Andalucía.
Tel: 01453 834 137 (UK).
www.Andalucian-adventures.co.uk
Walking Wild Andalucía
Walking around Roman roads, picturesque villages and unspoilt landscapes.
Tel: 951 16 00 49.
www.walkingwildAndalucia.com

INDOOR PURSUITS
Flamenco
Flamenco Dance Holidays
Tel: (020) 7099 4816 (UK).
www.danceholidays.com
Viva Flamenco
Holidays, workshops and classes.
Tel: 07850 22 31 33 (UK).
www.vivaflamencopromotions.com

Food and drink
The Atelier
Vegetarian and vegan hotel offering cookery courses by award-winning chef Jean-Claude Juston in this hamlet.
Mecina Fondales, Alpujarras.
Tel: 958 85 75 01.
www.ivu.org/atelier
Experience Box
Tel: 952 88 55 97.
www.experienceboxspain.com

Food and drink

Andalucía's landscape and climate have won an unrivalled reputation for the region's food and drink. Several Spanish classics originate here, and its restaurant owners have recently been making inroads into that preserve of French and more northerly establishments, the Michelin and other guides.

WHAT TO EAT AND DRINK

Andalucía is the home of *gazpacho*, the tomato-based chilled vegetable soup, and *rabo de toro*, the oxtail stew that might be considered the consummate Andalucian *plato*. The region's fishing fleets have access to two oceans, and its vegetable growers have turned its eastern half into a giant hothouse for subtropical fruit and vegetables, and the western half into lush cereal-growing areas and farmland.

With the exceptions of Jerez de la Frontera and Montilla, Andalucía was a late starter in the wine sector, but it has produced several whites and now a number of reds that are winning plaudits from critics. Málaga's modest Larios distillery produces a world-class gin that many aficionados prefer over well-known British brands.

Vegetarian and vegan foods

Most fair-sized towns have a vegetarian restaurant and many of the better restaurants will, forewarned, cater even for vegans. It's best to double-check vegetarian-sounding dishes, as they can sometimes be flavoured with ham or cod, or with animal stock.

Typical meals and ingredients

Specialities can vary from region to region, even village to village, but Andalucian farmers' perseverance with traditional methods produces fresh meats and vegetables wherever you eat or shop. Below are some typical foods you'll encounter across Andalucía.

Aceitunas olives. *Verdes* (green) or *negras* (black), and sometimes *rellenas* (stuffed).

Aguacate avocado.

Ajo blanco chilled white garlic soup.

Albondigas meatballs.

Alcachofas artichokes.

Almejas clams, often *a la marinera* (in white wine and herbs).

Almendras almonds, found in desserts such as *tarta* (flan), or sometimes as part of a sauce for *pollo* (chicken).

Alubias large white beans.

Anchoas anchovies. Also known as *boquerones.*

Apio celery.

Atún tuna, famously from the Costa de la Luz, often *al horno* (oven baked), or in *ensalada mixta* (mixed salad).

Bacalao cod: *a la plancha* (grilled), *frito* (fried), or in stews and soups.

Berenjenas aubergine.

Besugo bream.

Calabacín and **calabaza** courgette/ marrow, and pumpkin.

Calamares squid, often *fritos, a la romana,* or *en su tinta* (cooked in its own ink).

Cangrejo crab.

Cerdo pork.

Champiñones and **setas** mushrooms, a frequent tapa. *Champiñones* are commonly the larger button variety, *setas* wild woodland fungi.

Chorizo spicy red sausage.

Chuletas chops, of *cordero* (lamb) or *cerdo* (pork).

Codorniz quail. *Huevos de codornices* (quail's eggs) are a delicious tapa.

Conejo rabbit, commonly served as an *estofado* (stew), with *garbanzos* (chickpeas).

Croquetas breaded potato croquettes *rellenas* (stuffed) with chicken, ham or *espinaca* (spinach).

Espárragos asparagus.

Guisantes green garden peas.

Habas broad beans.

Huevos eggs: *duros* (hardboiled), *fritos* (fried), *revueltos* (scrambled, usually with something else) or *rancheros,* in a spicy tomato sauce with chorizo and *alubias.*

Lechuga lettuce.

Lenguado sole.

Lentejas lentils.

Mariscos seafood, but more correctly shellfish.

Merluza hake.

Morcilla a robust country sausage similar to black pudding.

Pato duck.

Pavo turkey.

Pechuga de pollo chicken breast.

Perdiz partridge.

Pez espada swordfish.

Pulpo and pulpito octopus and baby octopus.

Queso cheese: not an Andalucian strong point, but country-made *queso de cabra* (goat's cheese) is a great *tapa.*

Rape monkfish.

Raya skate.

Sardinas sardines. A typical way to cook these is to barbecue them on skewers, *al espeto.*

Solomillo better-quality beef steak.

Sopa soup.

Ternera veal, commonly in *patas* (leg of), or *estofado* (stew), or with *alubias* (beans).

Tortilla omelette. A Spanish staple in bars everywhere, and a good stopgap for vegetarians.

Sardines *al espeto*

Food and drink

WHERE TO EAT

Andalucians eat late by the rest of Europe's standards. Lunch, the main meal of the day, is from 2pm onwards. After an afternoon *merienda* around 5–7pm, which can be something savoury but usually sweet, dinner falls between 9pm and 11pm.

Restaurants in Andalucía vary from the humble beach bar or *chiringuito* serving barbecued fish almost straight out of the sea, to starched temples of haute cuisine in Seville, Granada and Córdoba. Prices generally vary according to the pretensions of the owners, but they are not always a guarantee of quality.

When choosing a restaurant the best advice is to eat where the locals eat and try to avoid anywhere that displays photographs of its dishes outside. Some rural *ventas* and roadside truck stops serve excellent *menús del día* at a price you couldn't argue with – a full car park is usually a guarantee that you will eat well within. No restaurant imposes a dress code on its

View from a riverside café on the Costa de la Luz

clientele, but if you don't want to feel out of place, dress casual-smart for any mid-price to expensive restaurant.

In the following list of recommended restaurants, the price symbols indicate the approximate cost per head of a typical meal without drinks:

★   up to €18
★★   €18–30
★★★   over €30

Seville

El Kiosco de las Flores ★★
A Triana institution, on the riverside, this is one of the places to taste fish in Seville.
Calle Betis.
Tel: 954 27 45 76.

La Albahaca ★★★
This converted mansion with film-set interiors has an excellent if expensive traditional menu.
Plaza Santa Cruz 12.
Tel: 954 22 07 14.
www.andalunet.com/ la-albahaca

Corral del Agua ★★★
Stylish courtyard restaurant in an alley by the Alcázar walls, with a menu veering towards

nueva cocina.
Callejón del Agua 6.
Tel: 954 22 48 41.
www.corraldelagua.es

Egaña Oriza ★★★
One of the smartest restaurants in town, with a *nueva cocina* menu (boar with pears and prunes), on a corner of the Alcázar gardens and Plaza Don Juan de Austria. The wonderful tapas bar is highly recommended.
Calle San Fernando 41.
Tel: 954 22 72 54. www. restauranteoriza.com

Enrique Becerra ★★★
Unassuming backstreet tapas bar and restaurant popular with locals and the *New York Times* food pages.
Calle Gamazo 2.
Tel: 954 21 30 49.
www.enriquebecerra.com

Hostería del Laurel ★★★
Busy and popular traditional restaurant below the eponymous hotel in a square in Santa Cruz. Baked meats and fish are a speciality, with an excellent *friturada variada* (batter-fried seafood selection).
Plaza de los Venerables 5.
Tel: 954 22 02 95. www.

hosteriadellaurel.com

Taberna del Alabardero ★★★
Another impressive mansion conversion, with an international menu.
Calle Zaragoza 20.
Tel: 954 50 27 21.

Cádiz and Costa de la Luz

Cádiz

Bar Jamón ★★
Serves traditional food, a good selection of tapas and home-made speciality breads.
Variante El Puerto-Rota, Glorieta Molino Platero, El Puerto de Santa María.
Tel: 956 85 05 13.
www.barjamon.com

El Sardinero ★★
Handsomely positioned, this is a favourite snack and takeaway restaurant for great fish, and the nearest *gaditanos* get to English takeaway fish and chips.
Plaza San Juan de Dios 4.
Tel: 956 26 59 26.

El Faro ★★★
Possibly the most fabulous fish restaurant in Andalucía, and certainly the most fabled. Book for the

pricier upstairs restaurant, or just roll up for the friendly downstairs tapas bar, and some wonderful variations on fish and seafood in either.
Calle San Felix 15.
Tel: 902 21 10 68.
www.elfarodecadiz.com

Ventorrillo el Chato ★★★
Dating in parts from the 1780s, this is said to have been the place where tapas was invented, and in the 1820s was King Fernando VII's favourite restaurant.
Vía Augusta Julia.
Tel: 956 25 00 25. www.
ventorrilloelchato.com

Sanlúcar de Barrameda
Casa Bigote ★★★
The place to taste Sanluqueña food: a seafront bar and restaurant in the traditional Bajo de Guía fishermen's *barrio* from which there is a view across the water to Doñana National Park.
Bajo de Guía.
Tel: 956 36 26 96. www.
restaurantecasabigote.com

Mirador Doñana ★★★
This upmarket neighbour to the Bigote has a less funky take on Sanlúcar's traditional fish and seafood.
Bajo de Guía.
Tel: 956 36 42 05.
www.miradordonana.com

Tarifa
Arte Vida ★★
Hotel-restaurant-gallery just north of Tarifa, with a beach restaurant specialising in grilled fish, meats, salads and pizzas.
Carretera N340, Km 79.3.
Tel: 956 68 52 46. www.
hotelartevidatarifa.net

Casa Amarilla ★★
Classic Andalucian *bodega* specialising in local ham, tuna and cheese in the centre of Tarifa's Sancho IV party zone.
Sancho IV El Bravo 9.
Tel: 956 68 19 93.
www.lacasaamarilla.net

Hurricane
Restaurante ★★★
Probably the best restaurant on the Tarifa beach, set in the dense subtropical gardens of the trendy Hurricane Hotel.
Hotel Hurricane,
Carretera N340.
Tel: 956 68 49 19.
www.hotelhurricane.com

Pueblos Blancos and Valle de Grazalema
Grazalema
La Garrocha ★★
This restaurant in the rainiest village in Spain uses ingredients from the Sierra de Cádiz, which include lamb chops with truffles and a great selection of fresh vegetables like asparagus and *tagarniñas* (wild thistles).
Plaza de España 8.
Tel: 956 13 23 76.
www.grazalemahotel.com

Ronda
Puerta Grande ★★
This relatively new arrival in a restaurant-heavy town has subtle variations on salmon in leek sauce, and *berenjenas con miel* (fried aubergine with honey).
Calle Nueva 10.
Tel: 952 87 92 00. www.
restaurantepuertagrande.
com

Pedro Romero ★★★
Ronda's shrine to bullfighting with real bulls' heads on the walls and photographs of Hemingway and Welles

hanging out with bullfighting heroes such as Antonio Ordoñez. The menu is somewhat upmarket, but it's still the place to try classics such as *rabo de toro*, *perdiz* and *conejo*.
Virgen de la Paz 18.
Tel: 952 87 11 10.
www.rpedroromero.com

Tragabuches ★★★
Unbeaten the length and breadth of Andalucía, this temple of *nueva cocina* goes from strength to strength and has a Michelin star for its unique combination of local ingredients and traditional dishes mixed in outrageous new ways.
José Aparicio 1.
Tel: 952 19 02 91.
www.tragabuches.com

Western Costa del Sol

Antequera
Los Dolmenes ★★
Convenient before or after visiting the dolmens on the edge of town, with a cool dining room in which local food is served.
Cruz El Romeral.
Tel: 952 84 59 56.

Benaoján
El Molino del Santo ★★★
This restaurant has one of the most idyllic settings in the whole of Andalucía: under willow trees by a mill stream in the gardens of a mountain-hideout hotel. Offers a wide range of local specialities using organic ingredients, with plenty to please every taste.
Barriada la Estación.
Tel: 952 16 71 51.
www.molinodelsanto.com

Gaucín
La Fructuosa ★★
The cosy dining room, arranged around an old wine press, extends on to the patio from which there are views of Gibraltar and the African coast.
Calle Convento 67.
Tel: 952 15 10 72.
www.lafructuosa.com

Gibraltar
Lord Nelson ★★
The best of the restaurants in the town centre.
10 Casemates Square.
Tel: 350 50009.
www.lordnelson.gi

The Rib Room ★★★
The elegant restaurant of the Rock Hotel has marvellous views, live music and an excellent wine list.
The Rock Hotel.
Tel: 350 73000. www.rockhotelgibraltar.com

Málaga
El Vegetariano de la Alcazabilla ★★
Fairly smart vegetarian restaurant handy for the Picasso Museum and the Alcazaba, with vegan dishes available.
Pozo del Rey 5.
Tel: 952 21 48 58.

Antonio Martín ★★★
One of Málaga's oldest fish restaurants, and one of the most expensive.
Plaza la Malagueta 16.
Tel: 952 22 73 98.
www.restauranteantoniomartin.com

Marbella
Il Cantuccio ★
Hidden in an alleyway off Calle Ancha, this great little Italian restaurant is one of Marbella's best-kept secrets.

Food and drink

Callejón Santo Cristo 3.
Tel: 952 77 04 92.

La Comedia ★★★
Pan-global dishes – from the Arctic Circle to Macronesia – served with style and wit in this trendy but friendly designer restaurant hidden in a corner of one of the *casco antiguo*'s old squares. Open for dinner only. Booking advised.
Puente Ronda 3.
Tel: 952 77 64 78.

Eastern Costa del Sol
Almería
Los Mariscos ★
Sturdy beer-and-tapas fish bar-restaurant – the place to eat with the locals.
Calle Mendez Nuñez 20.
Tel: 950 23 54 02.

Café Alcazar ★★
One of the most popular bar-restaurants in the Puerta Purchena district at the heart of the Old Town, with a wide range of seafood tapas and *platos* on offer.
Paseo de Almería 2.
Tel: 950 23 89 95.

Mesa España ★★
One of the best mid-range restaurants in Almería, offering fish, meat and vegetarian alternatives.
Calle Mendez Nuñez 19.
Tel: 950 27 49 28.

Taberna Torreluz ★★
A great central place for tapas and drinks, and the most informal of the three restaurants linked to the hotel of the same name.
Plaza Flores 3.
Tel: 950 23 43 99.

Valentin ★★★
Probably the most upmarket restaurant in town, with an extensive menu of delicately prepared fish and seafood dishes, and a complement of meat and international dishes.
Tenor Iribarne 19.
Tel: 950 26 44 75.

Cómpeta
El Pilón ★★
British-owned restaurant serving a filling and good-value *menú del día* on its terrace, with views over the rooftops and the surrounding hills. Good choices for vegetarians.
Calle Laberinto 3.
Tel: 952 55 35 12.

Granada and Sierra Nevada mountains
Granada
Arrayanes ★★
One of the best North African restaurants in the Albaicín, Arrayanes is sumptuously decorated and specialises in *tagines*, sturdy meat, fish or vegetable stews.
Cuesta Marañas 4.
Tel: 958 22 84 01.
www.rest-arrayanes.com

Cuñini ★★★
Serving excellent seafood from Andalucía and also Galicia, this smart restaurant off Bib-Rambla also has a cheap and friendly tapas bar.
Plaza Pescadería 14.
Tel: 958 25 07 77. http:// cuninigranada.iespana.es

Parador de San Francisco ★★★
A place to splash out and enjoy almost unrivalled views of the Albaicín from the garden terrace.
Real de la Alhambra.
Tel: 958 22 14 40.
www.parador.es

Pilar del Toro ★★★
Classic *granadino* dishes in this elegant, converted 17th-century mansion,

which has a downstairs tapas bar and upstairs restaurant with its own terrace.
Hospital de Santa Ana 12 (just off Plaza Nueva).
Tel: 958 22 54 70.

Las Tinajas ★★★
One of Granada's smartest restaurants, with a mix of southern and northern Spanish classics, and some fine fish dishes. Also handy for Bib-Rambla.
Calle Martínez Campos 17.
Tel: 958 25 43 93. www. restaurantelastinajas.com

Northern Andalucía
Córdoba
Almudaina ★★
One of the finest of Córdoba's restaurants, and the place to try some of the most typical Córdoban dishes, *rabo de toro* (oxtail) and *salmorejo* (a thick vegetable soup or stew).
Plaza Campo Santo de los Mártires 1.
Tel: 957 47 43 42. www. restaurantealmudaina.com

El Caballo Rojo ★★★
The most famous restaurant in the city,

specialising in local dishes dating from Moorish times, many of which still influence modern Andalucian cooking. The cheaper/ quicker tapas bar is also recommended.
Calle Cardenal Herrero 28.
Tel: 957 47 53 75.
www.elcaballorojo.com

El Churrasco ★★★
This smart restaurant completes Córdoba's trio of top-notch restaurants, and is famed for its titular pork dish, *churrasco*, in a pepper sauce.
Calle Romero 16.

Tel: 957 29 08 19.
www.elchurrasco.com

Úbeda
El Marqués ★★★
This restaurant is in one of Úbeda's two smartest hotels, a 16th-century mansion conversion. The menu specialises in traditional *Úbense* recipes using local meat and vegetables, and fish from the coast.
Hotel María de Molina, Plaza del Marqués 2.
Tel: 953 75 72 55.
www.hotel-maria-de-molina.com

The dining room of Córdoba's venerable eatery El Caballo Rojo

Accommodation

Andalucía is the most popular tourist destination in Spain and both the number and quality of hotels are increasing to meet that demand. Some more industrial cities such as Huelva and Málaga are still poorly served with visitor accommodation, while some of the smallest pueblos *now boast international-quality boutique hotels.*

Booking is advisable whenever possible, and an absolute must if you plan to visit during Semana Santa, or any other local festivity.

Hotels will hold rooms until 8pm or later if you warn them of your estimated arrival time, but some may require pre-booking by credit card. Be warned that many do not quote prices inclusive of 16 per cent IVA, Spain's value-added tax. Checkout is usually at noon, but most hotels will keep bags or even let you use the room until later, if asked.

Prices

Below is a selection of mid-range to higher-priced hotels across Andalucía which can be assumed to have en-suite facilities and take most credit cards. For information on hostels and camping, *see pp185–6.*

The prices shown according to the star system below are average summertime prices (although many hotels have year-round prices) for a double room. Suites and rooms will be extra during premium periods.

★	under €80
★★	€81–120
★★★	€121–150
★★★★	over €150

SEVILLE PROVINCE
Seville
Simón ★★
Friendly and popular mid-price option. An 18th-century mansion conversion, this is often busy all year.
Calle García de Vinuesa 19. Tel: 954 22 66 60. www.hotelsimonsevilla.com

Las Casas de los Mercaderes ★★★
One of the best-situated hotels in this noisy city, on a pedestrian street a short walk from the cathedral.
Calle Álvarez Quintero 9–13.
Tel: 954 22 58 58.
www.intergrouphoteles.com

Doña María ★★★
Handsomely remodelled town house.
Don Remondo 19.
Tel: 954 22 49 90. www.hdmaria.com

Hostería del Laurel ★★★

A hotel in the heart of Santa Cruz, above a popular restaurant.
Plaza de los Venerables 5.
Tel: 954 22 02 95.
www.hosteriadellaurel.com

San Gil ★★★

Away from the centre, this is a pleasant renovation of a 1901 town house with a courtyard, gardens and pool.
Calle Parras 28. Tel: 954 90 68 11.
www.sevillahotelsangil.com

Los Seises ★★★

A stunning renovation of a 16th-century palace in the shadow of La Giralda.
Calle Segovias 6. Tel: 954 22 94 95.
www.hotellosseises.com

Las Casas de la Judería ★★★–★★★★

Exquisitely refurbished mansion, in parts dating back to the 16th century.
Plaza de Santa María la Blanca, Callejón de Dos Hermanas 7. Tel: 954 41 51 50.
www.intergrouphotels.com

Casa Número 7 ★★★★

This small, intimate hotel is actually a private home, lovingly decorated with artefacts from the family art collection.
Calle Virgenes 7. Tel: 954 22 15 81.
www.casanumero7.com

Carmona

Alcázar de la Reina ★★

One of Carmona's fabulous 16th-century mansions, sumptuously renovated and sensitively modernised.
Plaza de Lasso 2. Tel: 954 19 62 00.
www.alcazar-reina.es

The *parador* in Carmona

La Casa de Carmona ★★★

Gorgeous 16th-century palace conversion in the beautiful town centre, decorated with antiques and paintings.
Plaza de Lasso 1. Tel: 954 19 10 00.
www.casadecarmona.com

CÁDIZ AND COSTA DE LA LUZ
Cádiz

Francia y Paris ★★

The best mid-range option in the old town, a central, quiet, if anonymous modern hotel behind a beautiful belle époque façade.
Plaza de San Francisco 6.
Tel: 956 21 23 19. www.hotelfrancia.com

Playa Victoria ★★★★

Best of the beachside hotels in central new Cádiz, with stylish rooms and suites, all with sea views.
Glorieta Ingeniero la Cierva 4.
Tel: 956 20 51 00.
www.palafoxhoteles.com

Conil de la Frontera
Fuerte Conil ★★★★

Part of the Fuerte chain, which has hotels in Marbella and Grazalema, this is the most comfortable of the Costa de

la Luz beach hotels, a large complex above the beach with pools and restaurants. Very popular with German and British visitors.
Playa de la Fontanilla. Tel: 956 44 33 44. www.fuertehotels.com

Jerez de la Frontera
Avenida Jerez ★★
Large, modern, convention-type hotel on one of Jerez's major boulevards, a short walk from the centre.
Avenida Alcalde Domecq 10.
Tel: 956 34 74 11. www.nh-hotels.com
Doña Blanca ★★
Probably the best mid-range option in Jerez, a pleasant modern hotel in a backstreet just metres from Jerez's busy central market.
Calle Bodegas 11. Tel: 956 34 87 16.
www.hoteldonablanca.com

Jimena de la Frontera
El Anón ★
Hotel-restaurant, built around a warren of tiny courtyards, with a rooftop pool.

Tarifa's Hurricane gardens, with pool and sea beyond

Calle Consuelo 34–40. Tel: 956 64 01 13. www.hostalanon.com

Sanlúcar de Barrameda
Posada de Palacio ★★★
A short walk from the town centre, an elegantly renovated 17th-century palace, built around a central courtyard.
Calle Caballeros 11.
Tel: 956 36 48 40.
www.posadadepalacio.com
Tartaneros ★★★
A grand mansion from Sanlúcar's wealthier days, in a central town square, decorated with antiques.
Tartaneros 8. Tel: 956 38 53 93.
www.hoteltartaneros.com

Tarifa
Arte Vida ★★★
Funky beach hotel, gallery and restaurant, just north of town.
Carretera N340, Km 79.3.
Tel: 956 68 52 46.
www.hotelartevida.com
Casa Amarilla ★★★
Stylish early 19th-century apartment hotel with individually designed suites.
Sancho IV El Bravo 9.
Tel: 956 68 19 93.
www.lacasaamarilla.net
Hurricane ★★★★
Notoriously difficult to book into, but with comfortable if simple rooms, beautiful gardens and pool.
Carretera N340, Km 78.
Tel: 956 68 49 19.
www.hotelhurricane.com

PUEBLOS BLANCOS AND VALLE DE GRAZALEMA
Arcos de la Frontera
Marqués de Torresoto ★★★

More historic splendour in this renovated mansion with a patio overlooking the view.
Calle Marqués de Torresoto 4.
Tel: 956 70 07 17.
www.hotelmarquesdetorresoto.com

Benarrabá
Banú Rabbah ★

Launched as a collective by young people from this tiny Pueblo Blanco, located between Ronda and Gaucín. Twelve rooms, some with views over the mountains, all with spacious terraces.
Calle Sierra Bermeja. Tel: 952 15 02 88.
www.hbenarraba.es

Grazalema
Puerta de la Villa ★★★

This is a stylishly renovated mansion hotel with spectacular views, restaurant, sauna and gym.
Plaza Pequeña 8. Tel: 956 13 23 76.
www.grazalemahotel.com

Casa de las Piedras ★★★★

Excellent if modest hotel, with a fine restaurant and a friendly atmosphere.
Calle las Piedras 32. Tel: 956 13 20 14.
www.casadelaspiedras.net

Ronda
Arriadh ★★

Five-room hotel, with gardens, pool and great views.

De-stress in style at Fuente de la Higuera

Camino de Laura.
Tel: 952 11 43 70.
www.andalucia.com/arriadh

Alavera de los Baños ★★

Ronda's most charming hotel: a row of 19th-century tanners' cottages converted into a Hispano-Arabic-styled hotel with a terrace restaurant and pool.
Calle San Miguel. Tel: 952 87 91 43.
www.alaveradelosbanos.com

San Gabriel ★★

This 18th-century mansion was the first hotel in Ronda's *casco antiguo*, renovated with great care by the Peréz family, who are gracious hosts.
Calle Marqués de Muctezuma 19.
Tel: 952 19 03 92.
www.hotelsangabriel.com

Acinipo ★★★

This mixes avant-garde design with classic Spanish décor, and is ideally situated away from traffic and with excellent mountain views.
Calle José Aparicio 7. Tel: 952 16 10 02.
www.hotelacinipo.com

La Cazalla ★★★

A short drive or cab ride out of Ronda, on a Roman road in its own secret valley, this incomparable little hotel has just six suites, all individually designed. Great food, wild gardens and a 12th-century plunge pool. Children are not allowed. Minimum stay two nights.
Tajo del Abanico, 4km (2½ miles) from Ronda. Tel: 952 11 41 75.
www.lacazalladeronda.com

Fuente de la Higuera ★★★★

This sumptuously renovated country house outside Ronda is run more as a help-yourself house party.
Partido de los Frontones. Tel: 952 11 43 55. www.hotellafuente.com

El Juncal ★★★★

Cool, minimalist designer hotel, a former *cortijo* (farmhouse) transformed with great style under the aegis of Tragabuches. Sauna and a wild, sloped walk-in pool.
Carretera Ronda–El Burgo.
Tel: 952 16 11 70. www.eljuncal.com

Véjer de la Frontera

Convento San Francisco ★

Converted convent at the heart of this gorgeous Pueblo Blanco.
La Plazuela. Tel: 956 45 10 01.
www.tugasa.com

La Casa del Califa ★★

The folks from Tarifa's Hurricane have restyled this beautiful old property into an elegant boutique hotel.
Plaza de España 16.
Tel: 956 44 77 30.
www.lacasadelcalifa.com

Zahara de la Sierra

Marqués de Zahara ★★

This friendly family-run mansion conversion is the best-kept secret among the Pueblos Blancos.
Calle San Juan 3. Tel: 956 12 30 61.
www.marquesdezahara.com

WESTERN COSTA DEL SOL

Benaoján

El Molino del Santo ★★★

Very pleasant English-owned country-house hotel, with bungalow-type rooms in mature gardens, an outdoor pool and lovely restaurant under willows by a tumbling mountain stream.
Estación de Benaoján/Montejaque.
Tel: 952 16 71 51.
www.molinodelsanto.com.
Closed: mid-Nov–mid-Feb.

Gaucín

La Fructuosa ★★

Five elegant modern suites with large terraces looking down towards the Rock and Africa.
Calle Convento 67. Tel: 952 15 10 72.
www.lafructuosa.com

Casablanca ★★★★

Handsome mansion conversion with gardens, pool and mock-Arabic *mirador.*
Calle Llana 12. Tel: 952 15 10 19.
www.casablanca-gaucin.com

Gibraltar

Eliott ★★

The smartest central hotel, popular with business travellers.

Governor's Parade. Tel: 350 70500.
www.eliotthotel.com

Caleta ★★★★

Luxury hotel on the beach in this
former fishing village at the other end
of the Rock.
Catalan Bay. Tel: 350 76501.
www.caletahotel.com

The Rock ★★★★

The Gibraltarian institution, built by
the Marquess of Bute in 1929. All
rooms have a sea view and there are
restaurants, bars and a pool.
Europa Road. Tel: 350 73000.
www.rockhotelgibraltar.com

Málaga

Las Vegas ★★

A decent Alameda-area option, close to
the beach; modern and purpose-built,
with its own pool.
Paseo de Sancha 22. Tel: 952 21 77 12.
www.hotellasvegasmalaga.com

Don Curro ★★★

This is one of the best hotels in Málaga:
simple, modern and comfortable, set
back from the busy Alameda.
Calle Sancha de Lara 7.
Tel: 952 22 72 00.
www.hoteldoncurro.com

Marbella

El Faro ★★

The best budget option in town: a
simple, friendly, purpose-built apart-
hotel on a quiet street between the
beach and the main street.
Calle Virgen del Pilar 11.
Tel: 952 77 42 30. www.hotelfaroinn.com

La Morada Más Hermosa ★★★

Best mid-range hotel in Marbella,
prettily renovated in the old town with
just five individually decorated suites
around a tiny courtyard.
Calle Montenebros 16.
Tel: 952 92 44 67.
www.lamoradamashermosa.com

El Fuerte ★★★★

On its own *avenida*, rooms have partial
or full sea views; there are two pools, a
gym and spa, and a beach club.
Avenida el Fuerte. Tel: 952 92 00 00.
www.fuertehotels.com

Marbella Inn ★★★★

Slightly more comfortable than
El Faro, with restaurant and
rooftop pool.
Calle Jacinto Benavente 16.
Tel: 952 82 54 87.
www.hotelmarbellainn.com

EASTERN COSTA DEL SOL
Almería

La Perla ★★

Almería's oldest hotel, now refurbished,
and a friendly budget option.
Plaza del Carmen 7. Tel: 950 23 88 77.
www.githoteles.com

Vincci Mediterráneo ★★

The trendiest hotel in Almería, with
rooms and public spaces verging on
minimalist style. Business facilities are
available.
Avenida del Mediterráneo 281.
Tel: 950 62 42 72. www.vinccihoteles.com

AM Torreluz ★★★

This is one of the smartest hotels in
the city. All mod cons, gym, sauna,

spa and small rooftop terrace with pool.

Plaza Flores 5. Tel: 950 23 43 99. www.torreluz.com

Gran Hotel Almería ★★★

Large four-star convention-type hotel dating from the 1960s. Restaurant, bars, pool, but in a noisy part of town.

Avenida Reina Regente 8. Tel: 950 23 80 11. www.citymar-hoteles.com

GRANADA AND SIERRA NEVADA
Bubión

Las Terrazas ★

Spartan but comfortable and friendly family-run hotel with views to the south of this Alpujarran village.

Plaza del Sol 7. Tel: 958 76 30 34. www.terrazasalpujarra.com

Granada

Juan Miguel ★★

Central hotel, near the Puerta Real, and a decent mid-range option.

Acero del Darro 24. Tel: 958 52 11 11. www.hoteljuanmiguel.com

Reina Cristina ★★

Handy central mid-price hotel in a fairly quiet side street. Another restored mansion, this is famous for being the last abode of the poet Lorca, who was arrested here and executed after the fall of the Republic. (Lorca's room was where room No 310 is now.)

Tablas 4. Tel: 958 25 32 11. www.hotelreinacristina.com

America ★★★

This is the ideal place to stay in Granada, a lovely old mansion deep inside the Alhambra. Booking ahead advised.

Real de la Alhambra 53. Tel: 958 22 74 71. www.hotelamericagranada.com

Carmen de Santa Inés ★★★

Like its sister hotel, the Palacio de Santa Inés, this is an exquisitely refurbished mansion, with suites off a column-lined courtyard with fountain.

Placeta Porras 7. Tel: 958 22 63 80. www.carmensantaines.com

Macià Plaza ★★★

Pleasantly modernised town-house hotel on this central square.

Plaza Nueva 5. Tel: 958 22 75 36. www.hotelplazagranada.com

Palacio de Santa Inés ★★★

Renovated 16th-century mansion at the bottom of the Albaicín, with rooms around a beautiful courtyard.

Cuesta de Santa Inés 9. Tel: 958 22 23 62. www.palaciosantaines.com

Triunfo ★★★

Smart, modern hotel at the far end of Gran Vía, quieter than some of the more central hotels.

Plaza del Triunfo 19. Tel: 958 20 74 44.

Guadix

Pedro Antonio Alarcón ★

Guadix is close enough to Granada or Almería to make it a day's round trip, but if you want to share the cave-life

experience, this unique hotel offers cave suites, gardens and pool.
Barriada San Torcuato.
Tel: 958 66 49 86. www.cuevas-pedro-antonio-de-alarcon.com

NORTHERN ANDALUCÍA
Baeza
Campos de Baeza ★
A favourite hotel among business travellers. It has two restaurants and an excellent view from its terrace.
Puerta de Córdoba 57. Tel: 953 74 73 11. www.hotelcamposdebaeza.com

Cazorla
Villa Turística de Cazorla ★★
Very pleasant hotel just on the edge of this mountain town, a short walk from the centre, with restaurant, gardens, pools and views of the town.
Ladera de San Isicio. Tel: 953 71 01 00. www.villacazorla.com

Córdoba
González ★
Former Moorish palace by the Mezquita, with rooms looking on to a whitewashed interior patio.
Calle Manrique 3. Tel: 957 47 98 19. www.hotel-gonzalez.com

El Triunfo ★
Probably the best mid-price option here, a friendly, traditional hotel on the eastern side of the Mezquita, with bar and restaurant and some rooms with Mezquita views.
Calle Corregidor Luis de la Cerda 79. Tel: 957 49 84 84. www.htriunfo.com

Amistad Córdoba ★★
Tastefully modernised conversion of two 18th-century mansions on the edge of La Judería, the former Jewish *barrio*, with a Mudéjar-style patio.
Plaza de Maimónides 3.
Tel: 957 42 03 35. www.nh-hotels.com

Las Casas de la Judería ★★★★
A renovated town mansion in front of the Alcázar, in the historic Jewish quarter, with spacious, bright and peaceful rooms.
Tomás Conde 10. Tel: 957 20 02 95. www.casasypalacios.com

Jaén
Europa ★★
A central hotel, renovated with contemporary décor.
Plaza de Belén 1. Tel: 953 22 27 04. www.husa.es

Condestable Iranzo ★★★
Another modern and comfortable hotel in the town centre.
Paseo de la Estación 32. Tel: 953 22 28 00. www.hotelcondestableiranzo.es

Úbeda
María de Molina ★★
Beautifully renovated 16th-century mansion with enclosed patio and incredible views.
Plaza del Ayuntamiento. Tel: 953 79 53 56. www.hotel-maria-de-molina.com

Palacio de la Rambla ★★★
Authentic 16th-century *palacio* on the edge of Úbeda's old town.
Plaza del Marqués 1. Tel: 953 75 01 96. www.palaciodelarambla.com

Practical guide

Arriving and getting around
Entry formalities

Visitors from EU countries, Iceland and Norway can enter Spain with a valid national identity card, although visitors from countries without ID cards, such as Britain, need a valid passport. Citizens of Australia, Canada, New Zealand and the USA do not need visas if they are staying for no more than 90 days. If you are coming from another country you need to apply for a visa before you leave.

Anyone planning to stay in Spain for more than 90 days should report to the police to register their presence. If you intend to live and work in Spain, you will need to go through the official channels so that you are registered with the Spanish employment, tax and welfare systems.

By air

Andalucía has five major international airports – Almería, Granada, Jerez de la Frontera, Málaga and Seville – plus the 'offshore' option of flights into Gibraltar. Málaga is by far the easiest international option, with flights from around Europe, North Africa and North American hub airports, as well as international connections via Madrid. Both Seville and Granada have regular international services, and Almería is expanding its network of air connections. Spain's national airline, **Iberia** (*tel: 902 400 500; (UK) 0870 609*

0500. www.iberia.es), operates national and international routes out of them all.

Seville's **San Pablo** airport (*tel: 902 40 47 04*) is 12km (7 miles) northeast of the city and a simple journey by car, taxi or bus (*half-hourly*) to the centre. Buses stop at **Santa Justa** railway station, which has connections to all Andalucian cities and most towns (*www.tussam.es*) (*see p182*).

Málaga's **Pablo Ruiz Picasso** airport (*tel: 902 40 47 04*) is 8km (5 miles) west of the city and the most easily accessible of all Andalucian airports. As well as taxis and buses (*half-hourly*) there is also a handy suburban train connection just a few minutes' walk from the airport and signed from the arrivals and departures halls. This line, the Málaga–Fuengirola line, has a half-hourly service in both directions and you should buy a ticket on the platform before you board. Anyone wanting to travel onwards by bus or train for long-distance routes should get off at Estación RENFE, one stop before the terminus at Centro/Alameda, as advised by the automatic announcements on the train. The Málaga–Fuengirola station is below the main RENFE station here, and both are a short walk away from the *Estación de Autobuses*.

Some UK budget airlines have regular flights to Andalucía. **Ryanair** (*www.ryanair.com*) flies to Málaga, Granada, Almería, Seville and Jerez de la Frontera. **easyJet** (*www.easyjet.com*)

flies to Almería and Málaga. **Thomas Cook** (*www.flythomascook.com*) organises flights to Málaga and, from May to October, to Almería.

By car

Visiting Seville and Andalucía from abroad by car is more an adventure than a comfortable option, but it is possible. Seville is roughly 600km (373 miles) from Spain's northern and southern borders with France, and a day's drive from Barcelona, Bilbao or Santander, which have handy ferry links to Britain (the last two being ports). *For details of ferry services, consult the Thomas Cook European Rail Timetable (see pp182–3 for details).*

Driving The best map (*see p186*) to negotiate Andalucía by any form of transport is the Michelin: Andalucía 1/400,000. Many first-time visitors to Andalucía are surprised at how mountainous much of it is, and although many of the roads are excellent this fact should be borne in mind when hiring and driving cars here. Similarly, a special warning has to be issued about the N340, the *autovía* (motorway) that skirts Andalucía's southern coastline. It is said to be the most dangerous motorway in Europe.

The Spanish drive on the right, along with most continental Europeans. Traffic offences can lead to on-the-spot fines and the police may even accompany you to an ATM. Seat-belt use is obligatory. Speed limits are 120km/h (75mph) on *autovías* (motorways), 90km/h (56mph) on other roads and 50km/h (31mph) in built-up areas. *Bandas sonoras* (speed bumps) are common in residential areas. Drink-driving is forbidden. Check cover for accident, theft of vehicle and liability with your travel insurer. The law requires that all cars carry a red warning triangle, replacement headlight bulbs and a reflective yellow jacket, which must be carried in the passenger compartment, for roadside emergencies.

There are two types of fuel widely available in all Spanish filling stations: unleaded petrol (*sin plomo*), with a choice of 95 or 98 octane, and diesel (*gasoil*). *Gasolineras* are plentiful in and on the outskirts of cities and towns, but grow scarce in the more remote countryside.

Car hire You will need to produce your passport and an EU or international driving licence to hire a car in Spain.

International companies such as **Avis** (*tel: 902 18 08 54. www.avis.es*), **Europcar** (*tel: 902 10 50 30. www.europcar.es*) and **Hertz** (*tel: 913 72 93 00. www.hertz.es*) have offices at all airports and in most city and town centres.

It is invariably cheaper and more convenient to pre-pay your car hire before you leave your country of departure.

Estación RENFE, Málaga

By coach

Coach (*autobús*) is the most popular and cheapest form of transport in Spain. These services are more frequent than trains and reach far more destinations.

Estaciones de autobuses are commonly found (and signed) on the perimeter of the city centre, such as Seville's **Prado de San Sebastián** (*tel: 954 41 71 18*) for southbound buses, and **Plaza des Armas** (*tel: 954 90 80 40*) for northbound and westbound services. The bus system is privatised, with as many as six or more different companies operating different routes, and they vary from city to city and town to town.

Pre-booking is possible only at bus stations and it is common to pay on board for all but long-distance routes. Be warned that bus services around weekends are often pre-booked by students returning home and families on the move.

By train

With sufficient time on your hands, trains are the most comfortable and scenic way to explore Andalucía. It is even possible to visit from northern Europe, although a journey from London or Paris would take two days.

Seville's **Santa Justa** railway station (*tel: 902 32 03 20*) is Andalucía's main rail terminus. The high-speed AVE train arrives here from Madrid via Córdoba. AVE trains also connect Madrid with Antequera and Málaga.

It's advisable to book ahead for intercity journeys, particularly in summer. If pre-booking is not possible, leave plenty of time to buy a ticket at the station. Anyone planning to travel around Andalucía should also check services and availability in advance. Spain's **RENFE** (Red Nacional de los Ferrocarriles Españoles) has a website (*www.renfe.es*) with information in Spanish and English, and a phone line (*tel: 902 24 02 02*). The phone line is Spanish, but there are operators fluent in English and other languages. Major travel agencies, Halcón Viajes and Viajes Marsans, have offices in all cities and towns and deal with domestic rail and coach travel as well as holidays. To make bookings before leaving home, contact **Rail Europe** (*US tel: 18006 228 600. www.raileurope.com; UK tel: 08448 484 064. www.raileurope.co.uk*).

The *Thomas Cook European Rail Timetable* is published monthly and gives up-to-date details of rail services and many ferry services throughout

Europe; this will help you plan your journey to Spain and around Andalucía. It is available to buy online from *www.thomascookpublishing.com*, at any branch of Thomas Cook in the UK or *tel: 01733 416477.*

Children

Children under four travel free on public transport. Young children in hotels often stay free, and older children at reduced rates, while family rooms with three or more beds are common in most hotels. Entry to state-owned museums is often free to under-18s, although some charge youth/student rates. There are sometimes reductions for under-12s, and special student rates for certain galleries, museums and concert halls.

Climate

Generally the east of Andalucía is much drier than the west with parts of Almería being desert. Although parts of the region get cold in winter and snow falls on the Sierra Nevada, on the coast it is possible to have breakfast outside in January. But as anywhere in the world these days, dramatic inversions of the climatic pattern are to be expected. Most commonly, Andalucía remains dry between May and September, with temperatures in the 20–30°C (70–90°F) range. Apart from the interior of Almería province and *la sartén* ('the frying pan'), around Écija east of Seville, temperatures rarely rise above 38°C (100°F), and this is usually a dry heat. Autumn weather

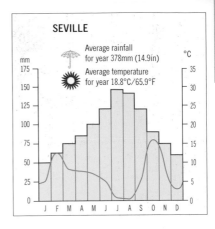

SEVILLE

Average rainfall for year 378mm (14.9in)

Average temperature for year 18.8°C/65.9°F

WEATHER CONVERSION CHART

25.4mm = 1 inch

$°F = 1.8 × °C + 32$

becomes unpredictable around late October, and the best advice to travellers packing with weather in mind is to take layers of clothing and a waterproof. If you are travelling from the coast into the interior and/or mountains, expect a temperature drop of 6°C (10°F) or more.

Crime

Crime is as common in Andalucía as it is in northern Europe. Most crimes are opportunistic, and Seville and Granada are known for the frequency of car break-ins and random bag snatches. However, common-sense behaviour with vehicles, valuables and personal safety should protect the visitor against all but the most unfortunate incidents. Park in secured pay parking or hotel car parks where possible, and remove all your valuables whenever and wherever you park. Don't carry expensive valuables around with you, and take care of obvious targets such as cameras and bags.

It is important, however, to maintain a sense of perspective: you are no more likely to be robbed or attacked here than anywhere else in Europe. Serious crimes are rare. If you are the victim of a crime, report it to the police as soon as possible, and enlist the help of hotels and others, if necessary.

Customs regulations

The duty-free allowance for visitors to Spain is: 200 cigarettes or 50 cigars, 1 litre of spirits or 2 litres of wine, 50 grams of perfume and 250 centilitres of toilet water. The limits for visitors travelling between EU countries are more generous but you should check your allowances before taking home large quantities of alcohol or tobacco. There is no limit on the amount of money you may bring into Spain, although sums of cash in excess of 6,000 euros must be declared.

Documents and insurance

Tourists need to carry their passport or national identity card with them at all times. Drivers should always ensure that they have their car papers with them.

Embassies and consulates

Almost every country has an embassy or consulate in Spain, usually in Madrid. Some, such as Britain, also have consulates in Fuengirola, Málaga

CONVERSION TABLE

FROM	TO	MULTIPLY BY
Inches	Centimetres	2.54
Feet	Metres	0.3048
Yards	Metres	0.9144
Miles	Kilometres	1.6090
Acres	Hectares	0.4047
Gallons	Litres	4.5460
Ounces	Grams	28.35
Pounds	Grams	453.6
Pounds	Kilograms	0.4536
Tons	Tonnes	1.0160

To convert back, for example from centimetres to inches, divide by the number in the third column.

MEN'S SUITS

UK	36	38	40	42	44	46	48
Rest of Europe	46	48	50	52	54	56	58
USA	36	38	40	42	44	46	48

DRESS SIZES

UK	8	10	12	14	16	18
France	36	38	40	42	44	46
Italy	38	40	42	44	46	48
Rest of Europe	34	36	38	40	42	44
USA	6	8	10	12	14	16

MEN'S SHIRTS

UK	14	14.5	15	15.5	16	16.5	17
Rest of Europe	36	37	38	39/40	41	42	43
USA	14	14.5	15	15.5	16	16.5	17

MEN'S SHOES

UK	7	7.5	8.5	9.5	10.5	11
Rest of Europe	41	42	43	44	45	46
USA	8	8.5	9.5	10.5	11.5	12

WOMEN'S SHOES

UK	4.5	5	5.5	6	6.5	7
Rest of Europe	38	38	39	39	40	41
USA	6	6.5	7	7.5	8	8.5

and Seville. Depending on your particular enquiry, it may be best to try Madrid before contacting a local office.

Embassies
Australia *Torre Espacio, Paseo de la Castellana 259D, planta 24, Madrid. Tel: 913 53 66 00. www.embaustralia.es*
Canada *Nuñez de Balboa 35, Madrid. Tel: 914 23 32 50. www.canada-es.org*
Ireland *Paseo de la Castellana, 46-4°, Madrid. Tel: 914 36 40 93.*
UK *Torre Espacio, Paseo de la Castellana, 259D, Madrid. Tel: 917 14 63 0. www.ukinspain.com*
USA *Serrano 75, Madrid. Tel: 915 87 22 00. www.embusa.es*

Consulates
Canada *Edificio Horizonte, Plaza Malagueta 3, Málaga. Tel: 952 22 33 46.*
UK *Américo Vespucio 5, Seville. Tel: 954 46 08 70; and Mauricio Moro Pareto, Edificio Eurocom, Málaga. Tel: 952 35 23 00.*
USA *Plaza Nueva 8-8, 29 planta E2-4, Seville. Tel: 954 21 87 51.*

Emergency telephone numbers
For all emergencies dial *112*, free of charge from any telephone, and ask for the service you require:
Ambulancia (ambulance)
Bomberos (fire brigade)
Policía (police)

Health and insurance
EU citizens are entitled to free emergency treatment in Spain, but some non-urgent treatments are only available privately, which is why it is important for all visitors to Spain to arrange private travel insurance to cover treatment and the costs of repatriation.

For British visitors, the European Health Insurance Card (EHIC) will cover most eventualities, but some treatments may require payment, which can be claimed back later. Non-urgent cases can be dealt with at a local *Centro de Salud* (Health Centre) during surgery hours.

The EHIC is available from *www.ehic.org.uk*, by phoning *0845 605 07 07* or from post offices.

There are no vaccine requirements to enter Spain.

Chemists
There is always one *farmacia* (chemist) *de guardia* open 24 hours a day in any district of a city and in most large towns, identified by a green cross above the entrance. Other chemists will display the address of the open chemist when they are closed. Chemists are allowed to diagnose minor ailments and prescribe certain over-the-counter drugs to treat these. Not all over-the-counter drugs (antihistamines, for example) are as freely available in Spain as elsewhere.

Hostels and camping
There are youth hostels for students and backpackers in most of the main cities of Andalucía (Seville, Granada,

Málaga, Almería, Huelva and Jerez de la Frontera), and also in Marbella, Sierra Nevada and Cazorla. For further information about youth hostels in Andalucía, contact the **Red Española de Albergues Juveniles** (*www.reaj.com*).

The climate in Andalucía is usually good for camping. For visiting Málaga and the Costa del Sol, there is a campsite in Marbella and another one in Ronda. South of Granada there is one site in Sierra Nevada and three in the Alpujarras (in Órgiva and Pitres), and near the sea are two in Motril.

The coast of Almería has a few campsites in Mojácar, Cabo de Gata and Roquetas de Mar.

For nature lovers there is a campsite in the Sierra de Cazorla (in Jaén province). For visiting Seville, there are campsites at Alcalá de Guadaira and Dos Hermanas. Cádiz has a selection of campsites near the coast in San Roque, Tarifa and Zahara de los Atunes. For further information about camping in Andalucía, contact the **Federación Española de Empresarios de Campings** (*www.fedcamping.com*) and the **Federación Andaluza de Campings** (*www.campingsandalucia.es*).

Maps

Tourist information offices distribute good free maps of their respective towns and cities. The best map shop in Andalucía is in the centre of Seville: **LTC** (*Avenida Menéndez Pelayo 42. Tel: 954 42 59 64. www.ltcideas.com*), just beyond the Jardines de Murillo

behind the Alcázar. In Britain, **Stanfords** (*12–14 Long Acre, London. Tel: 020 7836 1321. www.stanfords.co.uk*) also has branches in Bristol and Manchester. In the United States, try **Traveler's Choice** (*2 Wooster St, NYC. Tel: 212 941 1535. email: bookstore@turontravel.com*).

Media

International editions of British, continental European and US newspapers such as the *Wall Street Journal* and *Herald Tribune* are available on the day of publication in Seville and other larger cities and towns. Most larger and more upmarket hotels have satellite television.

Public holidays

Some public holidays are celebrated all over Spain; others are confined to Andalucía. In addition, every village, town and city has its own public holidays during the year.

1 January Año Nuevo (New Year's Day)
6 January Día de los Reyes (Epiphany)
28 February Día de Andalucía (regional holiday)
March or April (variable) Viernes Santo (Good Friday)
1 May Día del Trabajo (Labour Day)
15 August Asunción de la Virgen (Assumption of the Blessed Virgin Mary)
12 October Día de la Hispanidad (National Day of Spain)
1 November Todos los Santos (All Saints' Day)
6 December Día de la Constitución (Constitution Day)

8 December Inmaculada Concepción (Immaculate Conception)
25 December Día de Navidad (Christmas Day)

Sustainable tourism

Thomas Cook is a strong advocate of ethical and fairly traded tourism and believes that the travel experience should be as good for the places visited as it is for the people who visit them. That's why we firmly support The Travel Foundation, a charity that develops solutions to help improve and protect holiday destinations, their environment, traditions and culture. To find out what you can do to make a positive difference to the places you travel to and the people who live there, please visit *www.makeholidaysgreener.org.uk*

Time

Spain follows Central European Time, which is GMT (Greenwich Mean Time) plus one hour, or US EST (Eastern Standard Time) plus six hours.

Toilets

Public toilets are a rarity in Andalucía, as in the rest of Spain, although all department stores and public monuments have them. A café or bar is the best alternative. It is polite to buy a drink when making use of the facilities.

Tourist information

The responsibility for providing tourist information in Spain has been devolved to the regions, which in turn have devolved resources to each town and city. This makes it frustratingly difficult to get good information in advance of your visit, and so your best source is always the tourist information office on the spot. There are information posts at the major airports and railway stations.

Two good places to start planning a visit to Andalucía are Spain's national tourist website *www.spain.info* and the website of the regional government (Junta de Andalucía) *www.andalucia.org*. The Junta de Andalucía maintains a network of tourist information offices in the major cities, but some of them have a sparse supply of leaflets. Another useful, privately run site is *www.andalucia.com*

Seville's main tourist information office is at Plaza de San Francisco 19, next to the city hall (*tel: 954 59 52 88. www.turismosevilla.org*).

For information about Granada, see *www.granadatur.com*, and for Córdoba, see *www.turismodecordoba.org*

Travellers with disabilities

In Andalucía not many places specifically cater for disabled travellers. Most hotel and restaurant staff, however, will be willing to lend a hand to make someone in a wheelchair comfortable. Several organisations provide information about accessibility. In Spain contact **COCEMFE** (*Tel: 917 44 36 00. www.cocemfe.es*). In the UK the people to talk to are **Holiday Care** (*Tel: 0845 124 9971*) and **RADAR** (*Tel: 020 7250 3222. www.radar.org*).

Language

Many people working in hotels and restaurants will want to practise their English on you, but any attempt to speak Spanish will win you friends among the Spanish. Although in some respects it is a more complicated language than English, in one respect it is easier: words are pronounced as they look, according to a few simple rules.

PRONUNCIATION

Generally the accent falls on the second-to-last syllable unless it is marked with a written accent.

Vowel sounds

Vowels are always pronounced in the same way:

a	ah	**o**	oh
e	eh	**u**	oo
i	ee		

Consonant sounds

Consonants are the same as in English with the following exceptions:

ll like 'y' in 'yes'
rr is rolled, as pronounced in Scotland
h is silent
j like a guttural 'h'
g followed by 'e' or 'i' like a guttural 'h'
ñ like 'nio' as in 'onion'
v often sounds like a 'b'

BASIC WORDS AND PHRASES

	SPANISH
Hello	Hola
Goodbye	Adiós
Yes	Sí
No	No
Please	Por favor
Thank you	Gracias
You're welcome	De nada
Do you speak English?	¿Habla inglés?
I don't speak Spanish	No hablo español
Good day	Buenos días
Good night	Buenas noches
Excuse me	Perdón
Sir	Señor
Madam	Señora
How are you?	¿Cómo está?
Very well, thank you	Muy bien, gracias
My name is …	Me llamo …
What's your name?	¿Cómo se llama Usted?
How do I get to …?	¿Para ir a ….?
Where is …?	¿Dónde está …?
The underground/tube	El metro
The airport	El aeropuerto
The train station	La estación de tren

The bus	El bus
The street	La calle
A taxi	Un taxi
A hotel	Un hotel
The bathroom	Los aseos
A pharmacy	Una farmacia
A bank	Un banco
The tourist office	La oficina de turismo
What time is it?	¿Qué hora es?

EMERGENCIES

Help!	¡Socorro!
I am ill	Estoy enfermo/a
I am hurt	Estoy herido/a
The hospital	El hospital
A doctor	Un médico

DAYS AND MONTHS

Monday	lunes
Tuesday	martes
Wednesday	miércoles
Thursday	jueves
Friday	viernes
Saturday	sábado
Sunday	domingo
January	enero
February	febrero
March	marzo
April	abril
May	mayo
June	junio
July	julio
August	agosto
September	septiembre
October	octubre
November	noviembre
December	diciembre

NUMBERS

Zero	Cero
One	Uno
Two	Dos
Three	Tres
Four	Cuatro
Five	Cinco
Six	Seis
Seven	Siete
Eight	Ocho
Nine	Nueve
Ten	Diez

Index

Acknowledgements

Thomas Cook Publishing wishes to thank MICHELLE CHAPLOW/ANDALUCÍA SLIDE LIBRARY, to whom the copyright belongs, for the photographs in this book, except for the following images:

AFP/GETTY IMAGES/José Luis Roca 61
DREAMSTIME Nick Stubbs 1, sokolovski 40, Sabrina Dvihally 65, Michael Corrigan 89, Rechitansorin 149
FLICKR/PhillipC 142
ISTOCK PHOTOS Richard Goerg 80, Maverick Enterprises 107, Molloykeith 121
NICK INMAN 37, 43, 46, 49, 75, 92, 99, 105, 115, 120, 141, 145, 151, 159, 165
NICK STUBBS 122
PICTURE COLOUR LIBRARY Andalucia Plus 15, Ken Welsh 19, 51, 95, J.D. Dallet 62
THOMAS COOK PICTURE LIBRARY/Grant Rooney 156, Chris Willan 26, 54, 66, 83, 87, 153, 166
WORLD PICTURES 128, 161, 173

For CAMBRIDGE PUBLISHING MANAGEMENT LTD:
Project editor: Diane Teillol
Typesetter: Donna Pedley
Proofreaders: Jan McCann & Kelly Walker
Indexer: Marie Lorimer

SEND YOUR THOUGHTS TO BOOKS@THOMASCOOK.COM

We're committed to providing the very best up-to-date information in our travel guides and constantly strive to make them as useful as they can be. You can help us to improve future editions by letting us have your feedback. If you've made a wonderful discovery on your travels that we don't already feature, if you'd like to inform us about recent changes to anything that we do include, or if you simply want to let us know your thoughts about this guidebook and how we can make it even better – we'd love to hear from you.

Send us ideas, discoveries and recommendations today and then look out for your valuable input in the next edition of this title.

Emails to the above address, or letters to the traveller guides Series Editor, Thomas Cook Publishing, PO Box 227, Coningsby Road, Peterborough PE3 8SB, UK.

Please don't forget to let us know which title your feedback refers to!